FRUIT OF THE SPIRIT

Activity Book

Fruit of the Sprit Activity Book

All rights reserved. By purchasing this Activity Book, the buyer is permitted to copy the activity sheets for personal and classroom use only, but not for commercial resale. With the exception of the above, this Activity Book may not be reproduced in whole or in part in any manner without written permission of the publisher.

Bible Pathway Adventures® is a trademark of BPA Publishing Ltd.
Defenders of the Faith® is a trademark of BPA Publishing Ltd.

ISBN: 978-1-9992275-2-4

Author: Pip Reid

Creative Director: Curtis Reid

For more Bible resources, including Activity Books and printables, visit our website at:

www.biblepathwayadventures.com

◈◇ INTRODUCTION ◇◈

Children will LOVE learning about the Fruit of the Spirit with our hands-on *Fruit of the Spirit Activity Book*. Packed with easy-to-use lessons and fun and engaging activities to help children learn Godly character and how to demonstrate it in their daily lives. They'll discover the power of love through the parable of the Good Samaritan, experience the joy of Paul and Silas in prison as they praise in difficult circumstances, learn about peace through the faith of Daniel in the lions' den, explore patience as they follow Joseph's journey from the pit to the palace, and much more!

Bible Pathway Adventures helps educators teach children the Biblical faith in a fun and creative way. We do this via our Activity Books and Bible storybooks – all available on our website: shop.biblepathwayadventures.com.

Thanks for buying this Activity Book and supporting our ministry. Every book purchased helps us continue our work providing free discipleship materials to families and missions around the world.

The search for Truth is more fun than Tradition!

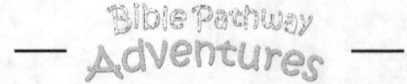

TABLE OF CONTENTS

Introduction 3
Fruit of the Middle East 8
Worksheet: Fruit of the Holy Spirit 9

Lesson One: Love 10
What's the Word: A lesson in love 12
Bible quiz: The good Samaritan 13
Bible word search puzzle: The good Samaritan 14
Worksheet: The good Samaritan 15
Newspaper worksheet: The Jericho Times 16
Coloring worksheet: If you love Me… 17
Worksheet: What did the Israelites wear? 18
Worksheet: The greatest commandment 19
Coloring page: Do everything in love 20
Creative writing: If you love Me 21

Lesson Two: Joy 22
What's the Word: Earthquake! 24
Bible quiz: Paul & Silas in prison 25
Bible word search puzzle: Paul & Silas in prison 26
Map activity: The Roman Empire 27
Bible word scramble: Why did the jailer rejoice? 28
Worksheet: Keeping our joy 29
Worksheet: Roman citizenship 30
Worksheet: Interview a jailer! 31
Coloring page: My spirit has rejoiced 32
Creative writing: Be joyful 33

Lesson Three: Peace 34
What's the Word: Surviving the den… 36
Bible quiz: Daniel and the lions 37
Bible word search puzzle: Daniel and the lions 38
Worksheet: Write your name in cuneiform 39
Worksheet: Into the lion's den 40
Worksheet: Finding peace in tough times 41

Worksheet: Peace 42
Bible verse puzzle: Who has great peace? 43
Coloring page: Peace 44
Creative writing: Trusting God brings peace 45

Lesson Four: Patience 46
What's the Word: Joseph rises to power 48
Bible quiz: Joseph 49
Bible word search puzzle: Joseph in Egypt 50
Coloring worksheet: Joseph's patience 51
Comprehension worksheet: Ancient Egyptian dreams 52
Worksheet: Patience 54
Coloring activity: Fruit of the Spirit 55
Coloring page: Romans 12:12 56
Creative writing: Patience and trust in Egypt 57

Lesson Five: Kindness 58
What's the Word: Kindness in action 60
Bible quiz: Healing a paralyzed man 61
Bible word search puzzle: Healing a paralyzed man 62
Newspaper worksheet: The Capernaum Times 63
Map activity: Land of Israel 64
Coloring worksheet: Healing a paralyzed man 65
Worksheet: Kindness 66
Worksheet: God's instructions 67
Worksheet: Choose kindness 68
Creative writing: Showing kindness 69

Lesson Six: Goodness 70
What's the Word: King Josiah 72
Bible quiz: King Josiah 73
Bible word search puzzle: Josiah reigns in Judah 74
Comprehension worksheet: High Places 75
Worksheet: Josiah restores the Passover 76
Bible word unscramble: Josiah 77
Worksheet: Goodness 78
Worksheet: Did You Know? 79
Coloring page: Goodness 80
Worksheet: I can show Goodness 81

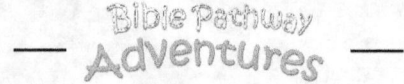

Lesson Seven: Faithfulness 82
What's the Word: A faithful servant 84
Bible quiz: Abraham 85
Bible word search puzzle: Abraham's faithfulness 86
Bible activity: Abraham's journey 87
Map activity: Footsteps of Abraham 88
Coloring worksheet: The call of Abram 89
Worksheet: Faithfulness 90
Worksheet: Interview Abraham! 91
Coloring page: Faithfulness 92
Creative writing: Faithfulness rewarded 93

Lesson Eight: Gentleness 94
What's the Word: Opposing authority 96
Bible quiz: Miriam and Aaron oppose Moses 97
Bible word search: The gentle leader 98
Worksheet: Who was Moses? 99
Worksheet: The tabernacle 100
Worksheet: My travel diary 101
Coloring worksheet: Be gentle… 102
Worksheet: Moses 103
Coloring page: Fruit of the Spirit 104
Worksheet: The power of gentleness 105

Lesson Nine: Self-control 106
What's the Word: Mercy in the wilderness 108
Bible quiz: David spares Saul's life 109
Bible word search: David spares Saul's life 110
Coloring worksheet: David's test of self-control 111
Comprehension worksheet: Who was King Saul? 112
Worksheet: Self-control 113
Bible verse puzzle: Do you have self-control? 114
Worksheet: Self-control superheroes! 115
Coloring page: Self-control 116
Worksheet: I can show self-control 117

Crafts & Projects

Bible craft: Make a hanging mobile	119
Bible craft: Fruit of the Spirit puppets	123
Bible craft: Make a door hanger	127
Bible craft: Make a fruit basket	133
Coloring page: Proverbs 21:21	141
Bible activity: Fruit of the spirit sequencing cards	143
Bible craft: Make a fruit of the spirit lapbook	147
Bible craft: Guess the Bible verse	155
Banner: Love	159
Banner: Joy	161
Banner: Peace	163
Banner: Patience	165
Banner: Kindness	167
Banner: Goodness	169
Banner: Faithfulness	171
Banner: Gentleness	173
Banner: Self-control	175
Answer Key	177
Discover more Activity Books!	184

Fruit of the Middle East

In ancient Israel, many different types of fruit grew in the land. But fruit was more than just food to the Hebrews - it was a symbol that appeared in their culture, names, proverbs, statutes and traditions. You can read all about these types of fruit in the Bible.

Fruit of the Holy Spirit

Read Galatians 5:22-23 and John 16:8.
The role of the Holy Spirit is to convict you of sin (1 John 3:4), which leads you into righteousness and sound judgment. Answer the statements below.

① I showed love when..

② I showed joy when..

③ I had peace when..

④ I showed patience when ....

⑤ I showed kindness when ....

⑥ I showed goodness when ....

⑦ I was faithful when ....

⑧ I showed gentleness by...

⑨ I showed self-control when ....

....

....

....

....

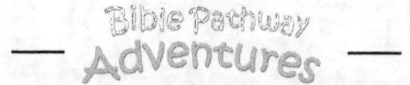

LESSON PLAN - LOVE

The good Samaritan: Luke 10:25-37

1. Introduction:

Begin the lesson by dividing students into pairs. Give each pair a simple task to complete (e.g. tying a shoelace or folding a piece of paper). One student in each pair can only use one hand, and their partner can only use the opposite hand. They must work together to complete the task. The goal is for pairs to co-operate and empathize with each other's limitations. After the game, ask students: "What if the person in need was someone you didn't like or didn't know? Would you still help?" Explain that today's lesson will focus on the parable of the good Samaritan, a story that explores this dilemma. During the lesson, encourage students to think about the choices each character made, and what this parable can teach us.

2. Review key vocabulary:

- **SAMARITAN:**
  a person from Samaria (a central region of Israel in biblical times)

- **JERICHO:**
  a city in ancient Israel

- **LEVITE:**
  an Israelite from the tribe of Judah, one of the 12 tribes of Israel

- **COMPASSION:**
  to show pity and concern for someone, and to act on it

- **LAW:**
  the Torah

3. Read Luke 10:25-37 from the Bible, or read the story below:

A teacher asked Yeshua (Jesus) a question, saying, "What should I do to inherit eternal life." Yeshua said to him, "What is written in the Torah?" He answered, "You shall love God with all your heart, with all your soul, with all your strength and with all your mind, and love your neighbor as yourself." The teacher then asked Yeshua, "Who is my neighbor?" Yeshua replied, "There was a man who traveled from Jerusalem to Jericho and fell among robbers. The robbers stripped him and beat him and left him half dead. A priest and a Levite both passed by on the other side. However, a Samaritan saw him and had pity on him. He bound up his wounds, gave him oil and wine, and put him on his own animal. He took him to an inn and took care of him, paying the innkeeper for any extra expenses. Which of these three men was a neighbor to the man," asked Yeshua. The teacher replied that the one who showed mercy was the neighbor. Yeshua said to him, "You go and do likewise."

4. Questions to encourage critical thought:

Contrast: How did the actions of the Samaritan differ from the priest and the Levite?
Analyze: Why do you think the Samaritan helped the injured man?
Explain: What can you learn from this parable about loving your neighbors and treating others with kindness and respect, regardless of your differences?
Describe: How did the good Samaritan show love in this story?

5. Memory verse:

"Love God with all your heart, with all your soul, with all your strength and with all your mind, and your neighbor as yourself." (Luke 10:27)

Did you know?

The distance between Jericho to Jerusalem is 15 miles (24 kilometers) with an elevation increase of about 3400 feet (1060 meters).

6. Activities:

* What's the Word: A lesson in love
* Bible quiz: The good Samaritan
* Bible word search puzzle: The good Samaritan
* Worksheet: The good Samaritan
* Newspaper worksheet: The Jericho Times
* Coloring worksheet: If you love Me…
* Worksheet: What did the Israelites wear?
* Worksheet: The greatest commandment
* Coloring page: Do everything in love
* Creative writing: If you love Me…
* Bible craft: Make a hanging mobile
* Banner: Love

A lesson in love

Read Luke 10:25-37 (ESV). Using the words below,
fill in the blanks to complete the Bible passage.

| NEIGHBOR | LEVITE | DENARII | ANIMAL |
| JERUSALEM | COMPASSION | MERCY | ROBBERS |

> The Torah teacher, desiring to justify himself said to Yeshua, "Who is my ....?" Yeshua replied, "A man was going down from .... to Jericho and fell among robbers, who stripped him, beat him and departed, leaving him half dead. Now by chance a priest was going down that road, and when he saw him he passed by on the other side. Likewise, a .... when he came to the place and saw him, passed by on the other side. But a Samaritan, as he journeyed, came to where he was and when he saw him, he had .... He bound up his wounds, pouring on oil and wine. Then he set him on his own .... and brought him to an inn and took care of him. The next day he took out two .... and gave them to the innkeeper, saying, 'Take care of him, and whatever more you spend I will repay you when I come back.' Which of these three do you think proved to be a neighbor to the man who fell among the ....?" He said, "The one who showed him ...." And Yeshua said to him, "Go and do likewise."

The good SAMARITAN

Read Luke 10:25-37. Answer the questions below.

1. Who asked Yeshua how to inherit eternal life?

2. How did Yeshua answer this man in Luke 10:27?

3. Where was the traveler going in the story?

4. What happened to the traveler on this road?

5. Who was the first man to walk past?

6. Who was the second man to walk past?

7. Who was the third man to see the traveler?

8. What did the Samaritan do to help the traveler?

9. How much did he pay the innkeeper?

10. When Yeshua asked the Torah teacher who was the neighbor, how did he answer?

The good SAMARITAN

Read Luke 10:25-37. Find and circle the words below.

```
L E R T J Q W H B W Y W E U Q
L I N M Q P O K E N J A B V L
M E M J E R I C H O U L T P O
N S V L A S J P Q Y W S N R V
M G A I D W S R C X I J B O E
D H F C T O P I T T S S P B S
I W W H Q E F E A K D M H B A
R Z M B U Z D S D H U E P E M
M B Q G V P X T M S Z R S R A
Z W O U N D Z O O T M C I O R
Q G O I W X V Q N E D Y M A I
C O D Q B F T Y F G S S X D T
F O R T U G G C L G T M L W A
P C T O R A H T E A C H E R N
D E N A R I I J X H R F F V L
```

WOUND
ROAD
LOVE
JERICHO
ROBBER
MESSIAH
SAMARITAN
PRIEST
MERCY
LEVITE
DENARII
TORAH TEACHER

The good Samaritan

Draw a picture of the good Samaritan.

If I met someone on the road who had been beaten and robbed, I would…

....
....
....
....
....
....
....
....
....
....
....

This parable teaches me…

....
....
....
....
....
....

If the parable of the good Samaritan was a book, the cover would look like this…

City of Jericho

The Jericho Times

LAND OF ISRAEL   A DISCIPLESHIP PUBLICATION

Bandits on road

....

....

....

....

....

....

Innkeeper wanted

Samaritan helps traveler

....

....

....

....

The good Samaritan

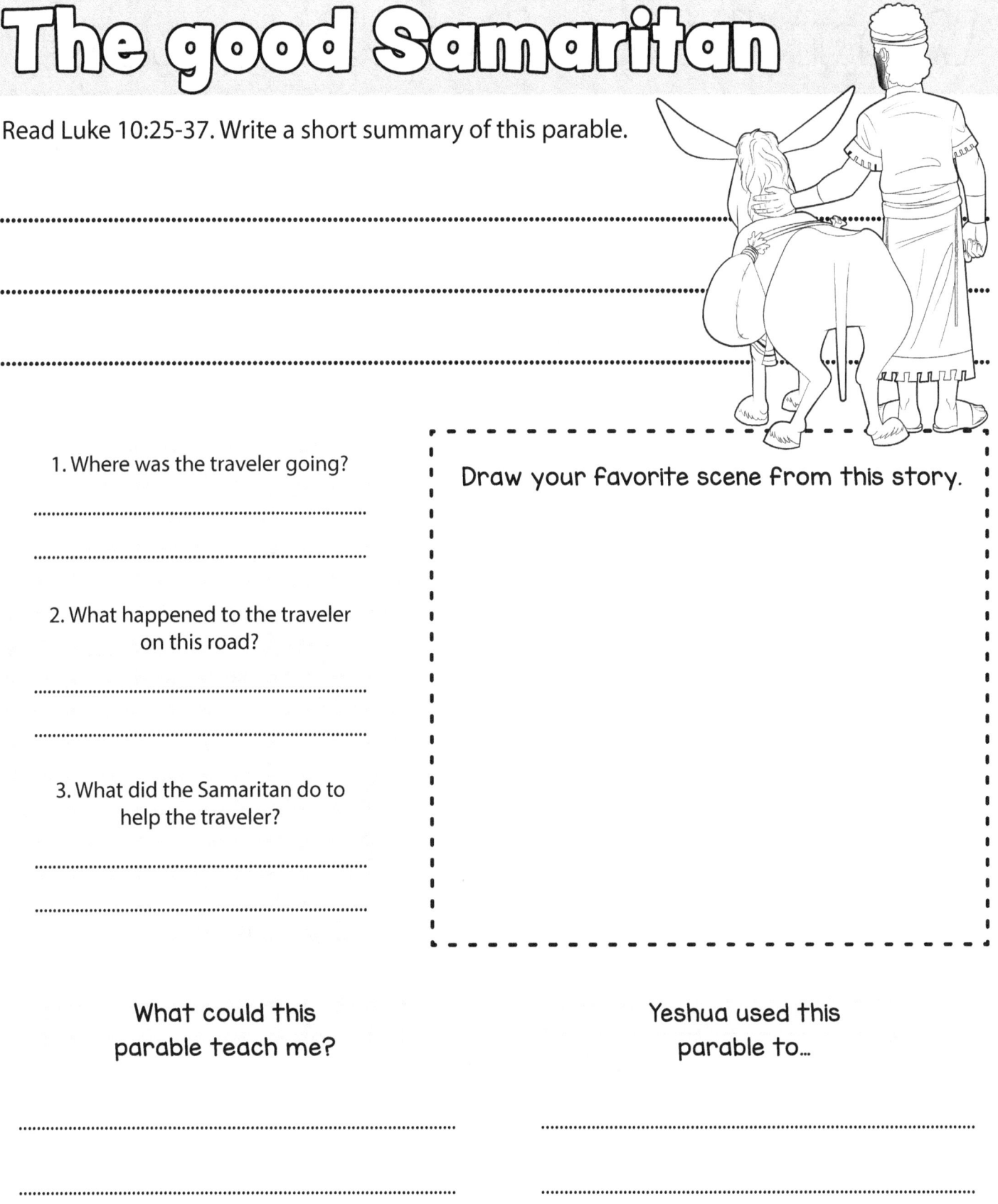

Read Luke 10:25-37. Write a short summary of this parable.

....

....

....

1. Where was the traveler going?

....

....

2. What happened to the traveler on this road?

....

....

3. What did the Samaritan do to help the traveler?

....

....

Draw your favorite scene from this story.

What could this parable teach me?

....

....

Yeshua used this parable to…

....

....

Fruit of the Spirit Activity Book

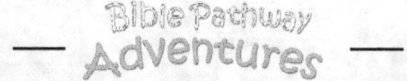

What did the Israelites wear?

During Bible times, Israelite men wore different clothes to the clothes men wear today. Most men wore an inner tunic, an outer robe or cloak, tzitzits, and sandals. Tunics were made from wool, linen or cotton, and held together at the waist by a belt made of leather or cloth. Outer robes were made of woolen cloth. Blue and white tzitzits made of linen or wool strands were worn to remind men to obey God's commandments (Numbers 15:37-41). Sandals were made of leather and dry grass, and had strings or ropes made of cheap materials. Using the Internet or an encyclopedia, research what men wore in Bible times. Write two facts about each item of clothing in the boxes below.

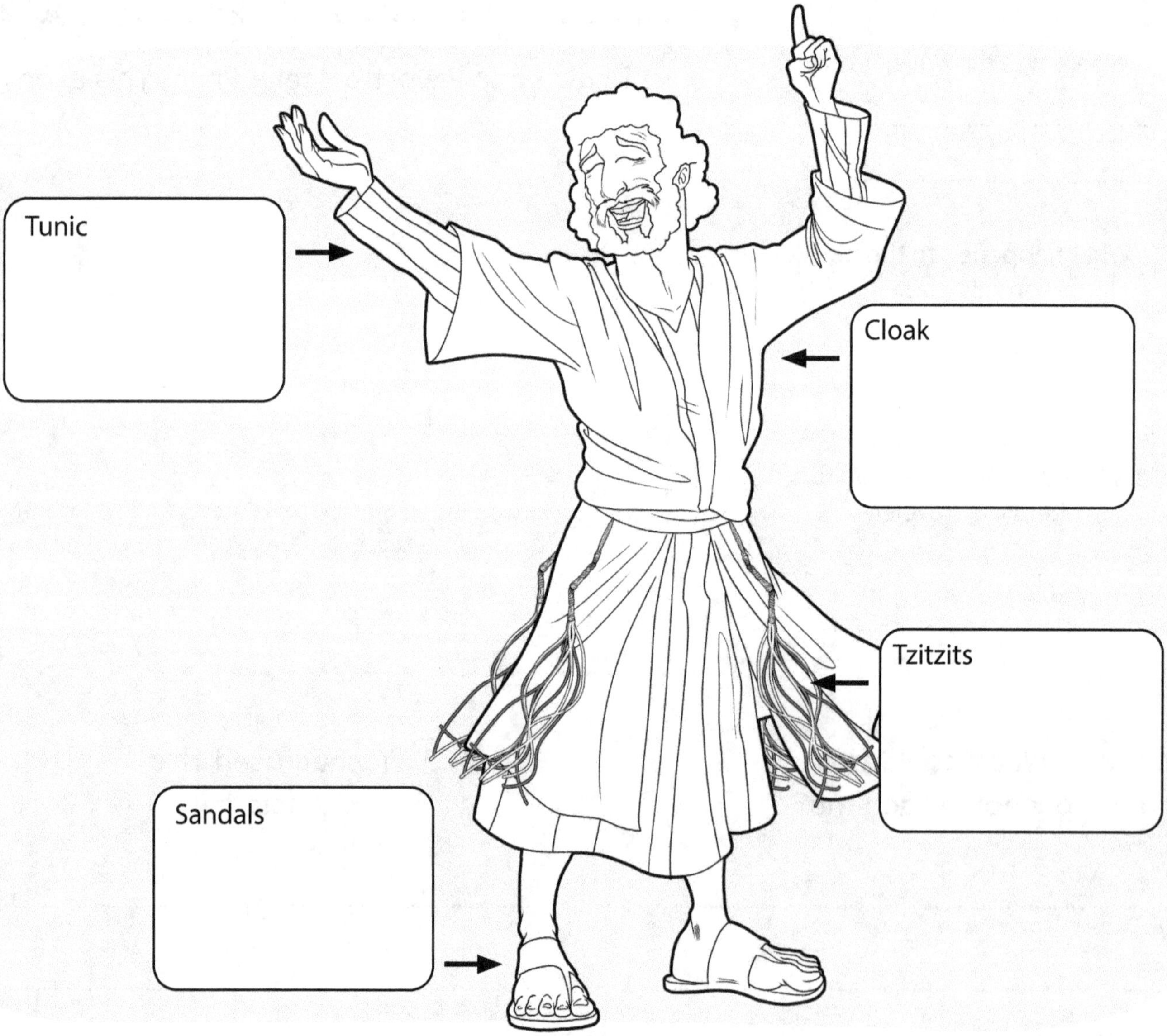

Tunic →

Cloak ←

Tzitzits ←

Sandals →

The greatest commandment

Read Matthew 22:1-46. Complete the worksheet below.

The greatest commandment is:

....

....

....

Who said it?

....

Who is my neighbor?

1. ....

2. ....

3. ....

Ways I show love to my neighbor:

....

....

I love God with all my heart, soul, and mind by:

....

....

If you love Me

"If you love me, you will keep my commandments. And I will ask the Father, and he will give you another Helper, to be with you forever, even the Spirit of truth, whom the world cannot receive, because it neither sees him nor knows him. You know him, for he dwells with you and will be in you. I will not leave you as orphans; I will come to you. Yet a little while and the world will see me no more, but you will see me. Because I live, you also will live. In that day you will know that I am in my Father, and you in me, and I in you. Whoever has my commandments and keeps them, he it is who loves me. And he who loves me will be loved by my Father, and I will love him and manifest myself to him." (John 14:15-21)

How do you love the Messiah? Write a short paragraph to describe how you love Him. Color the illustration at the bottom of the page.

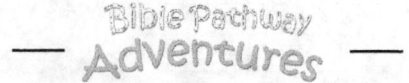

LESSON PLAN - JOY

Paul & Silas in prison: Acts 16:16-40

1. Introduction:

Begin today's lesson by asking students to use their imagination. Picture this: You're locked in a prison - it's dark, cold, and the hope for freedom seems bleak. In this situation, what would you do? Would you accept defeat, or would you choose to be joyful? Give students five minutes to write down their answer, and then discuss with the class. Explain that today's lesson will focus on two men who found themselves in this situation. Despite the harsh conditions, they chose to sing and fill their prison cell with praises to God.

2. Review key vocabulary:

- **PHILIPPI:** an important Greek city in Bible times, located in Asia Minor

- **PAUL:** a famous apostle who spread the teachings of the Messiah

- **SILAS:** a leader in the early church, friend of Paul

- **ROMANS:** rulers of the Roman Empire, people who came to rule parts of Europe, the Near East, and North Africa

- **MAGISTRATE:** a person who acts as a judge in law courts

3. Read Acts 16:16-40 from the Bible, or read the story below:

In Philippi, a slave girl with a spirit of divination followed Paul and Silas, shouting, "These are servants of the Most High God!" Annoyed, Paul exorcised her spirit, angering the girl's owners who were profiting from her. They seized Paul and Silas and dragged them into the marketplace. "These men are Jews and they are disturbing our city." The crowd joined in attacking them, and the magistrates threw them in prison. As Paul and Silas prayed and sang songs in prison, there was an earthquake and the prison doors flew open. Seeing this, the jailer nearly killed himself, thinking the prisoners had escaped. But Paul said, "Don't hurt yourself. We are all here." The jailer fell down before Paul and Silas. "What must I do to be saved?" he asked. Paul replied, "Believe in Yeshua the Messiah, and you will be saved." He shared the gospel with the jailer and all the people who lived in his house. That night, the jailer washed Paul and Silas' wounds. Then he and all his people were baptized. After this, the jailer took Paul and Silas home and fed them. When the magistrates heard that Paul and Silas were Roman citizens, they were afraid and asked them to leave the city.

4. Questions to encourage critical thought:

Contrast: Compare the magistrates' behavior before and after Paul and Silas were imprisoned.
Analyze: Why did the spirit of divination leave the slave girl?
Explain: Why do you think Paul and Silas experienced joy in prison?
Describe: How did Paul and Silas show joy in this story?

5. Memory verse:

"Rejoice in the Lord always. I will say it again: Rejoice!" (Philippians 4:4)

Did you know?

Paul was a Roman citizen (Acts 22:26-27). Because of this, he had the right to appear before Caesar, the Roman emperor.

6. Activities:

* What's the Word: Earthquake!
* Bible quiz: Paul & Silas in prison
* Bible word search puzzle: Paul & Silas in prison
* Map activity: The Roman Empire
* Bible word scramble: Why did the jailer rejoice?
* Worksheet: Keeping our joy
* Worksheet: Roman citizenship
* Worksheet: Interview a jailer!
* Coloring page: My spirit has rejoiced
* Creative writing: Be joyful
* Bible craft: Fruit of the Spirit puppets
* Banner: Joy

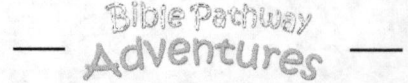

Earthquake!

Read Acts 16:25-34 (ESV). Using the words below, fill in the blanks to complete the Bible passage.

| MIDNIGHT | JAILER | PAUL | HOUSEHOLD |
| PRISONERS | DOORS | BAPTIZED | GOD |

❝ About …………………… Paul and Silas were praying and singing hymns to God, and the …………………… were listening. Suddenly there was a great earthquake and the foundations of the prison were shaken. Immediately all the …………………… opened and everyone's chains were unfastened. When the …………………… woke and saw that the prison doors were open, he drew his sword and was about to kill himself, thinking that the prisoners had escaped. But Paul cried with a loud voice, "Do not harm yourself, for we are all here." The jailer called for lights and rushed in. Trembling with fear, he fell down before …………………… and Silas. "What must I do to be saved?" And they said, "Believe in Yeshua the Messiah and you will be saved, you and your household." They spoke the word of …………………… to him and to all who were in his house. And the jailer took them and washed their wounds; and he was …………………… at once, he and all his family. Then he took them into his house and gave them food. And he rejoiced along with his entire …………………… that he had believed in God. ❞

Paul & Silas IN PRISON

Read Acts 16:16-40. Answer the questions below.

1. In which city were Paul and Silas thrown in prison?

2. To what piece of equipment were their feet fastened?

3. What did Paul and Silas do while they sat in prison?

4. What event opened the prison doors?

5. Why did the jailer want to kill himself?

6. Why did the jailer take Paul and Silas to his house?

7. Why did the jailer and his household rejoice?

8. Why were the magistrates afraid of Paul?

9. What did the magistrates do next?

10. Who did Paul and Silas visit before they left the city?

Paul & Silas IN PRISON

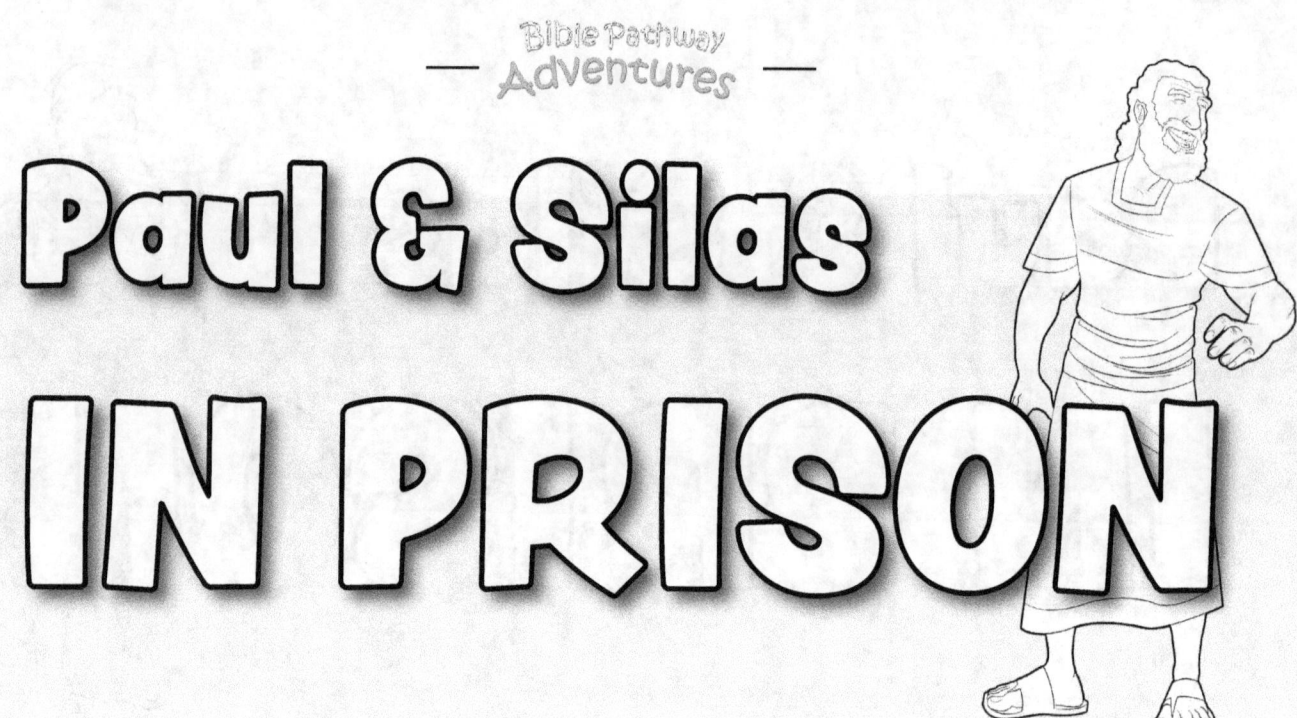

Read Acts 16:16-40. Find and circle the words below.

```
A Y N F T R N J O H P G L T A
P W R T H A Q W N O D B D Q E
R E S I L A S T U U F B C H V
D O A K R C P D P S G K Q F S
X F M R Q A O B R E K B L O I
M N B A T N C J I H N N G U N
Y V C X N H F X S O D F D N G
I B V H H Y Q V O L J I P D I
P H Y A D G T U N D G B K A N
P M A G I S T R A T E I N T G
Y U T U X P H O R K G Q B I K
Z Q U Z G A R P C F E U V O P
K F P H I L I P P I R U W N J
D O O R S F M C H A I N S S R
R R S W O R D B L R D J P F E
```

- SILAS
- MAGISTRATE
- SINGING
- PRISON
- CHAINS
- ROMAN
- HOUSEHOLD
- FOUNDATIONS
- SWORD
- PHILIPPI
- EARTHQUAKE
- DOORS

The Roman Empire

During the time of the apostle Paul, the Roman Empire was the world's superpower. Using the Internet or an historical atlas, research and draw the boundaries of the Roman Empire in the 1st – 2nd Century AD. Answer the questions below.

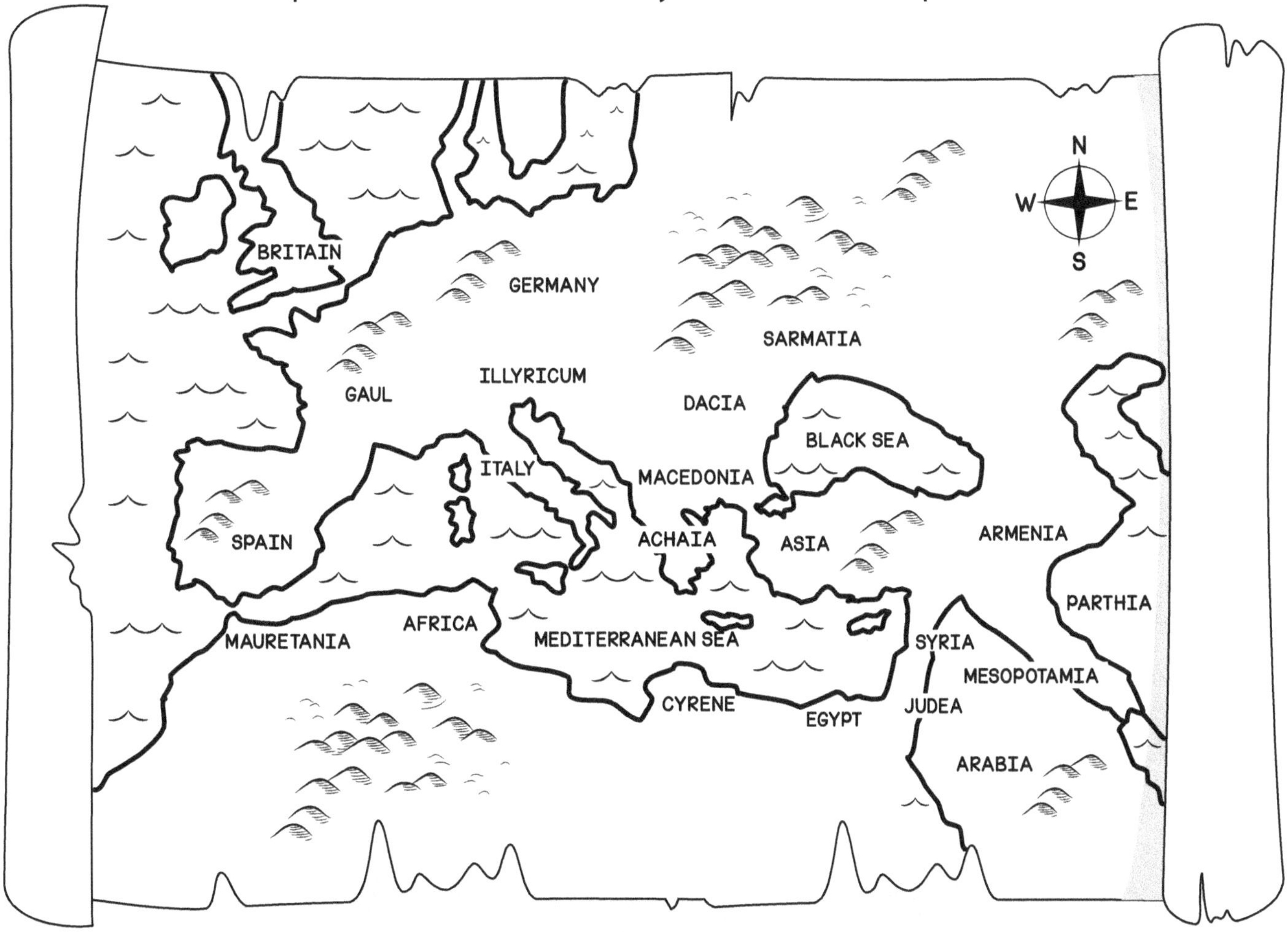

What three continents did the Roman Empire cover in the 1st - 2nd Century AD?

....

Using a modern map, list ten countries that were once part of the Roman Empire.

....

....

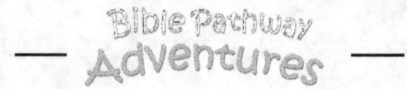

Why did the jailer rejoice?

Unscramble the words to find the answer. *Hint: Acts 16:34 (ESV).*

"dAn he oeejicrd aolng hitw ish

_____

teiern oeuhdlohs atht eh

_____

had dilevebe in doG."

_____

Keeping our joy

What does the Bible say about joy? How can you maintain your joy, even during tough times? Read and answer the questions below.

Read the Bible verses and write down what they say about joy:

Nehemiah 8:10: "...for the joy of the LORD is your strength."
....

Psalm 30:5: "...Weeping may stay for the night, but rejoicing comes in the morning."
....

Philippians 4:4: "Rejoice in the Lord always. I will say it again: Rejoice!"
....

Understanding joy in tough times:

What is joy?
....

How is joy different from happiness?
....

Why do you think the Bible tells us to find joy in hard times?
....

Keeping your joy

Write down the following Bible verses. Discuss how they suggest we can keep our joy in tough times.

Romans 12:12: ....

James 1:2-3: ....

John 16:33: ....

Roman citizenship

"Paul said to them, "They have beaten us publicly, uncondemned, men who are Roman citizens, and have thrown us into prison; and do they now throw us out secretly? No! Let them come themselves and take us out." The police reported these words to the magistrates, and they were afraid when they heard that they were Roman citizens. So, they came and apologized to them." (Acts 16:37-39)

For the first few centuries AD, Roman citizenship was a highly coveted prize. It was a privileged status given to freeborn individuals (not slaves). Although Paul was a Hebrew, he was born in the city of Tarsus, which was part of the Roman Empire at that time. His birth in Tarsus granted him Roman citizenship. Roman citizens were given a variety of rights that many others living in the Roman Empire did not have. For example, citizenship gave you the right to a fair legal trial, and the right to request Caesar to hear a case. Citizens who were condemned to death were spared from certain methods of execution. When the magistrates learned that Paul and Silas were Roman citizens, they apologized to them, and asked them to leave the city.

1. Why did Paul have Roman citizenship?

2. Read Acts 16:25-40. Why do you think the magistrates were afraid?

Color the Roman soldier!

Interview a jailer!

Paul and Silas were thrown in prison (Acts 16). The jailer put their feet in stocks so they could not escape. Imagine you are the jailer. A magazine has sent you a questionnaire. Tell them about this incident.

1. Introduce yourself.

....

2. Tell us about Paul and Silas.

....

....

3. Describe the earthquake.

....

....

4. Why did you start to believe in the Messiah?

....

....

"**My spirit has rejoiced in God my Savior.**"

(Luke 1:47)

Be Joyful...

Read Acts 16:25-40 and 1 Thessalonians 5:16-18. We can be joyful even when life is hard. Write a short paragraph to describe how you can be joyful in all circumstances.

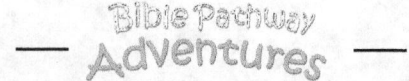

LESSON PLAN - PEACE

Daniel and the Lions: Daniel 6:1-28

1. Introduction:

Begin the lesson with a fun game. Write various core values (e.g. honesty, courage, kindness) on slips of paper. Fold these up and put them in a box. Explain to students that they're about to experience a small part of an ancient story. This story involves a man who had to stand firm in his beliefs, despite a terrifying situation. Divide students into small groups. One student from each group will take a slip from the box. That slip represents their core value. Tell each group to discuss how they would react if they were forced to deny their core value, under the threat of death. Would they stand firm, or would they deny their value to save themselves? Explain that today's lesson will focus on Daniel, a man who found himself in a similar situation.

2. Review key vocabulary:

- **BABYLON:** a city-state of ancient Mesopotamia (in present-day Iraq)
- **KING DARIUS:** the king of Babylon
- **SATRAP:** a provincial governor in the ancient Babylonian empire
- **TRUST:** to believe that someone is good and honest and will not harm you, or that something is safe and reliable
- **MALICIOUS:** not kind to someone, an action that causes hurt or pain to another person

3. Read Daniel 6:1-28 from the Bible, or read the story below:

King Darius appointed 120 satraps across his kingdom, along with three officials, including Daniel who worshipped Yahweh, the one true God. The satraps did not want to answer to Daniel, and decided to cause trouble. They said to the king, "Make a law that says everyone must pray to you as their god for the next 30 days. If they pray to another god, throw them to the lions." And the king agreed. When Daniel heard about the law, he kept praying to God. But the satraps were watching Daniel, and they told the king, "Daniel broke the law and prayed to his god. You said that anyone who disobeys this law must be punished." The king liked Daniel. He worked hard to save him, but he could not do so. Finally, he had Daniel thrown to the lions. "May your God deliver you!" he declared. Early the next morning, he rushed to the den to see Daniel. "Has your God saved you from the lions?" Daniel looked up, and said, "My God sent an angel to shut the lions' mouths so they didn't eat me. He knew I trusted Him and had done nothing wrong." The king's men pulled Daniel out of the den unharmed. Instead, the men who had accused him were thrown into the den.

4. Questions to encourage critical thought:

Contrast: How did the king's behavior differ before and after Daniel was thrown into the lions' den?
Analyze: Why was Daniel thrown into the lions' den?
Explain: How was Daniel able to survive a night with the lions?
Describe: How did Daniel demonstrate peace in this story?

5. Memory verse:

"You keep him in perfect peace whose mind is stayed on You, because he trusts in You." (Isaiah 26:3)

Did you know?

Daniel would have been at least 80 years old when he was thrown to the lions in Babylon.

6. Activities:

* What's the Word: Surviving the den…
* Bible quiz: Daniel and the lions
* Bible word search puzzle: Daniel and the lions
* Worksheet: Write your name in cuneiform
* Worksheet: Into the lion's den
* Worksheet: Finding peace in tough times
* Worksheet: Peace
* Bible verse puzzle: Who has great peace?
* Coloring page: Peace
* Creative writing: Trusting God brings peace
* Bible craft: Make a door hanger
* Banner: Peace

Surviving the den...

Read Daniel 6:16-23 (ESV). Using the words below,
fill in the blanks to complete the Bible passage.

| KING | PALACE | TRUSTED | LIONS |
| RING | ANGEL | DANIEL | SERVANT |

" The .... commanded and Daniel was brought and cast into the den of lions. The king declared to Daniel, "May your God whom you serve continually, deliver you!" And a stone was brought and laid on the mouth of the den, and the king sealed it with his own signet .... and with the signet ring of his lords, that nothing might be changed concerning Daniel. Then the king went to his .... and spent the night fasting and did not sleep. The next morning, the king hurried to the den of .... As he came near the den where Daniel was imprisoned, he cried out in anguish, "O Daniel, ... of the living God, has your God, whom you serve continually, been able to deliver you from the lions?" Then Daniel said to the king, "O king, live forever! My God sent His .... and shut the lions' mouths, and they have not harmed me, because I was found blameless before him; and also before you, O king, I have done no harm." Then the king was exceedingly glad, and commanded that .... be taken up out of the den. Daniel was taken up out of the den and no harm was found on him because he had .... in God. "

Daniel and the LIONS

Read Daniel 6:1-24. Answer the questions below.

1. Who was the king of Babylon?

2. What plans did the king have for Daniel in Daniel 6:3?

3. Why could the Magi not find any reason to complain about Daniel?

4. Who plotted to kill Daniel?

5. What happened to Daniel after he gave thanks to God by his open window?

6. Why was Daniel thrown to the lions?

7. Which king had Daniel thrown to the lions?

8. How was the lion's den sealed?

9. How was Daniel protected from the lions in the den?

10. Why was no harm done to Daniel in the lion's den?

Daniel and the LIONS

Read Daniel 6:1-24. Find and circle the words below.

```
D L N Z Y G O A V L G M K X L
E A P K T I V L A I D F I X S
M R N D E M Y D V V S U N R H
M L I I L J W S D I B R G I Z
B J N Y E S L I G N L J D B T
A Q A S O L E V O G A T O D M
K Z M N T L W Z T G M P M P K
F C U E G O N K K O E G B C B
E T P K P E N X M D L T T T W
B T H G L Q L E K J E U R Z A
D E N O F L I O N S S E U L N
P R A Y D B C Z D L S F S O M
P N B Q B N W P G P V E T Y H
Q Z G S M K R D A R I U S Z E
V A P E A C E H E B R E W Z X
```

DARIUS
HEBREW
KINGDOM
TRUST
DEN OF LIONS
BLAMELESS
PRAY
LIVING GOD
STONE
PEACE
ANGEL
DANIEL

Write your name in cuneiform

Cuneiform was developed by the Sumerians. It was the first system of writing, and included hundreds of pictographs. Because there were so many symbols, it was the job of a scribe to learn to read and write, and record laws, treaties, and religious customs. When Daniel lived in Babylon, this is how the Babylonians kept records.

Write your name in cuneiform:

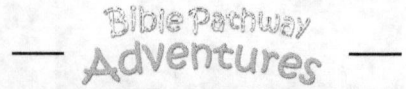

Into the lions' den

Daniel was thrown into a den of lions. Do you think he took anything with him? Think about life in Babylon and make a list of items you would take into a lion's den. Draw some of the items inside the bag. Use your imagination!

1. ....
2. ....
3. ....
4. ....
5. ....
6. ....
7. ....
8. ....
9. ....
10. ....

Finding peace in tough times

Read Daniel 6:1-28. Complete the worksheet below.

1. Story summary:

Write a short summary of Daniel 6:1-28 in your own words.

....

....

2. Questions:

What law did the king make that got Daniel in trouble?

How did Daniel respond when he heard about the law?

What happened to Daniel because he didn't obey the new law?

What was the result of Daniel's faith and peacefulness during his time in the lions' den?

3. Finding Peace in Tough Times:

Daniel stayed peaceful during his time in the lions' den because he trusted God. Can you think of a time when you felt scared or worried? What did you do? Write about it below:

....

....

....

....

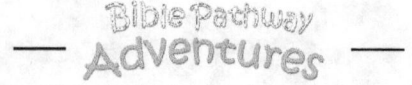

Peace

The story of Daniel and the lions teaches me…

....
....
....
....
....
....
....
....
....

Read Psalm 119:165. Great peace is promised to people who…

....
....
....
....
....
....
....
....
....
....
....

I know I have God's peace inside me when…

....
....
....
....
....
....

Draw a picture of Daniel in the lions' den.

Who has great peace?

This Bible verse is written in code. Use the chart at the bottom of the page to fill in the missing letters and crack the code!
Hint: Read Psalm 119:165 (ESV)

G R E A T P E A C E H A V E T H O S E W H O
17 26 10 5 16   20 10 5 13 10   22 5 4 10   16 22 3 25 10 14 22 3

L O V E Y O U R L A W ; N O T H I N G
12 3 4 10   8 3 11 26   12 5 14 ; 21 3 16 22 23 21 17

C A N M A K E T H E M S T U M B L E
13 5 21   6 5 1 10   16 22 10 6   25 16 11 6 9 12 10

A	B	C	D	E	F	G	H	I	J	K	L	M
5	9											

N	O	P	Q	R	S	T	U	V	W	X	Y	Z
	3											

"Turn away from evil and do good; seek peace and pursue it."

(Psalm 34:14)

Trusting God brings peace

Read Daniel 6:1-28. Complete the activities below.

Part 1: Story reflection

After reading or listening to Daniel 6, reflect on how Daniel trusted God in his situation.

Draw a picture in the box below showing peaceful Daniel in the lions' den, surrounded by peace because of his trust in God.

Part 2: Trusting God

What does it mean to trust God? Write down your thoughts here:

....
....
....

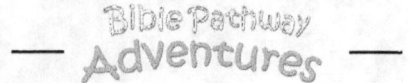

LESSON PLAN - PATIENCE

Joseph rises to power: Genesis 39:20-41:45

1. Introduction:

Divide the class into teams, and give each team a set of building blocks or puzzle pieces. Each team must work together to build a structure or solve a puzzle. One team member will be blindfolded, while other team members will give them instructions. Encourage the teams to practice patience by communicating calmly, listening carefully, and taking turns. The team that successfully completes the task while demonstrating patience is the winner! After the game, explain that today's lesson will focus on the story of Joseph, highlighting how his patience during tough times led to many opportunities and blessings.

2. Review key vocabulary:

- **JOSEPH:** one of Jacob's 12 sons

- **POTIPHAR:** an officer of Pharaoh

- **PHARAOH:** the king of Egypt

- **FAMINE:** a situation where there is not enough food for a great number of people

- **INTERPRET:** to decide what the intended meaning of something is

3. Read Genesis 39:20-41:45 from the Bible, or read the story below:

Joseph was sold into slavery in Egypt by his jealous brothers. There, he worked for Potiphar, an officer of Pharaoh, the king of Egypt. With God's help, Joseph was successful in everything he did. One day, Potiphar's wife tried to seduce him. "No!" said Joseph. "This is against what God wants." Instead, she falsely accused him to Potiphar, and in turn, he threw Joseph into prison. But Joseph did not lose hope. He patiently waited for God to help him. While in prison, Joseph used his gift for understanding dreams to help Pharaoh's cupbearer and baker. Sometime later, Pharaoh had two strange dreams that no one could explain. Remembering Joseph's gift of understanding dreams, the cupbearer told Pharaoh about him. Joseph was brought before Pharaoh, and he helped the king understand his strange dreams: Egypt would have seven years of plenty followed by seven years of famine. Pharaoh was impressed! He set Joseph free and made him the governor of Egypt.

4. Questions to encourage critical thought:

Contrast: How did Joseph's life change from the time he was in prison to becoming the governor of Egypt?
Analyze: Why do you think Pharaoh trusted Joseph to explain his dreams?
Explain: How did Pharaoh's dreams lead to Joseph's rise to power?
Describe: How did Joseph remain patient and strong during difficult times?

5. Memory verse:

"A patient person is very smart. A quick-tempered person makes mistakes." (Proverbs 14:29)

Did you know?

In Egypt there is an ancient artificial canal near the town of Medinet-el-Faiyum, called 'Bahr Yusuf'. This roughly translates from Arabic as the 'waterway of Joseph'.

6. Activities:

* What's the Word: Joseph rises to power
* Bible quiz: Joseph
* Bible word search puzzle: Joseph in Egypt
* Coloring worksheet: Joseph's patience
* Comprehension worksheet: Ancient Egyptian dreams
* Worksheet: Patience
* Coloring activity: Fruit of the Spirit
* Coloring page: Romans 12:12
* Creative writing: Patience and trust in Egypt
* Bible craft: Make a fruit basket
* Banner: Patience

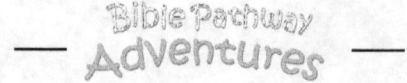

Joseph rises to power

Read Genesis 41:38-47 (ESV). Using the words below, fill in the blanks to complete the Bible passage.

SPIRIT	PHARAOH	CHARIOT	RING
THRONE	GOLD	JOSEPH	EGYPT

"Pharaoh said to his servants, "Where can we find a man like this who has the .... of God?" Then .... said to Joseph, "Since God has shown you all this, there is none so discerning and wise as you are. You shall be over my house and all my people shall order themselves as you command. Only as regards the .... will I be greater than you." And Pharaoh said to Joseph, "I have set you over all the land of ...." He took his signet .... from his hand and put it on Joseph's hand, clothed him in fine linen, and put a .... chain about his neck. And he made him ride in his second .... And they called out before him, "Bow the knee!" Thus Pharaoh set him over all the land of Egypt. Then Pharaoh said to ...., "I am Pharaoh and without your consent no one shall lift up hand or foot in the land of Egypt." And Pharaoh called Joseph's name Zaphenath-paneah and gave him in marriage to Asenath, the daughter of Potiphera, priest of On. So Joseph went out over the land of Egypt. He was thirty years old when he entered the service of Pharaoh, king of Egypt."

JOSEPH

Read Genesis 39:20-41:47. Answer the questions below.

1. Who threw Joseph in prison?

2. What did the prison warden do for Joseph?

3. Who did Pharaoh have thrown in prison?

4. How did Pharaoh celebrate his birthday?

5. Who told Pharaoh about Joseph in prison?

6. What did Joseph do for Pharaoh?

7. How did Pharaoh reward Joseph?

8. How old was Joseph when he began working for Pharaoh?

9. Who was Joseph's new wife?

10. In which land did this story take place?

Joseph in EGYPT

Read Genesis 39:20-41:45. Find and circle the words below.

```
R Q O M H M L J E O P W A A P
F M B N H H S O F V N W P A C
B A K E R Q M S N X F T A Z H
S K K H O O N E F P D K T H A
L O O U F O E P V K G N I E R
W C Q A I X F H T Q A M E B I
E Y U D R W X O M P U L N R O
F S Q P R E P R S O E A C E T
R A Q O B E I O Q T J V E W Z
G S M E X E A I S I L B U U C
J T U I P J A M O P K I Y J A
J K G F N T U R S H M Y T N I
E G Y P T E W F E A U W Y T N
P H A R A O H D Q R X G T C D
D K X N E F W W P R I S O N T
```

CUPBEARER

HEBREW

EGYPT

PATIENCE

POTIPHAR

PHARAOH

PRISON

JOSEPH

DREAMS

CHARIOT

FAMINE

BAKER

Joseph's patience

Read Genesis 41:46 and write the Bible verse below.

....

....

....

1. Which land did Pharaoh rule over?

....

....

2. Why did Pharaoh make Joseph governor of Egypt?

....

....

3. What gifts did Pharaoh give Joseph?

....

....

Draw your favorite scene from Genesis 41.

The life of Joseph teaches me…

....

....

I show patience when…

....

....

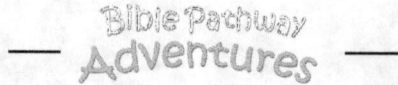

Ancient Egyptian dreams

This article explains the importance of dreams to the ancient Egyptians. Read the text and answer the questions on the next page.

Dreams

In ancient Egypt, dreams were considered divine predictions of the future. The Egyptians used their dreams to cure illnesses, make important decisions, and even to decide where to build a temple or when to fight a battle. Dreams were messages from the gods that foretold disasters or good fortune. For example, a deep well represented prison, a shining moon meant forgiveness, and a large cat symbolized a bumper crop.

The Egyptians often asked priests, magicians or professional dream interpreters to help them understand their dreams. But these interpreters didn't always agree, and similar dreams were sometimes given different meanings. The Egyptians were so interested in the meaning of their dreams they even had temples like the Temple of Horus in Edfu, where they would lie in 'dream beds' and hope to have a dream about advice, comfort or healing.

Many dreams were recorded on pieces of papyrus known as 'dream books'. From these books we know that some common images included breaking stones, teeth falling out, drowning in the Nile, drinking warm beer, and eating white bread. One of these dream books was discovered in the village of Deir el-Medina, near the Valley of the Kings. It contained a list of dreams describing activities such as pounding, brewing, weaving, sightseeing, stirring, and plastering. These dream records show the importance Egyptians placed on dreams. No wonder Pharaoh was pleased when Joseph explained his two dreams!

Ancient Egyptian dreams

Mission objective: To understand the importance of dreams to the ancient Egyptians. Read each question and write your answer on the lines below.

How did the Egyptians use dreams?

....

....

Why would the Egyptians lie in a 'dream bed'?

....

....

What can you find inside a 'dream book'?

....

....

Who gave Joseph the understanding to explain Pharaoh's dreams?

....

....

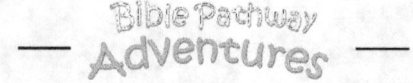

Patience

I can show patience toward my brother or sister by…

Read 1 Timothy 1:15-16. Who has perfect patience?

The story of Joseph teaches me…

Read Job 42:10. Draw Job being rewarded for his patience.

Fruit of the Spirit

Open your Bibles and read Galatians 5:22-23.
Write the Bible verses on the lines below. Color the fruit.

"
....
....
"
....

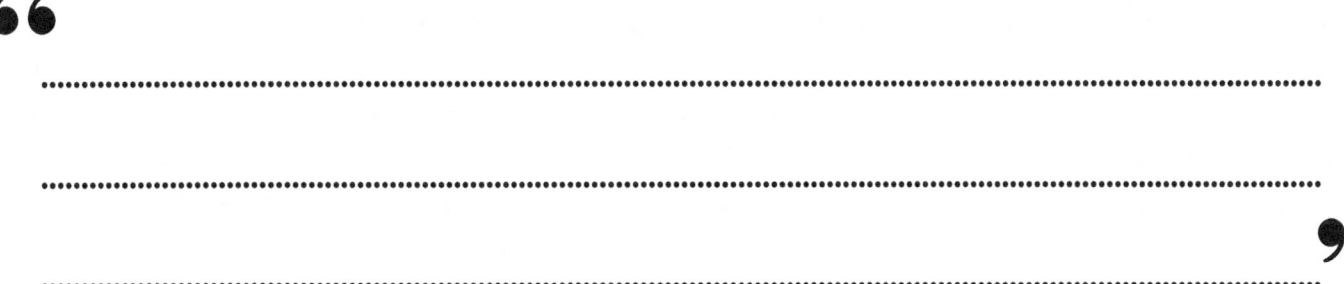

"**Rejoice in hope, be patient in tribulation, be constant in prayer.**"

(Romans 12:12)

Patience and trust in Egypt

Read Genesis 39:20-41:45. Complete the activities below.

Part 1: Story reflection

After reading or listening to the story of Joseph's rise to power (Genesis 39:20-41:45) reflect on Joseph's patience. Draw a picture of Joseph waiting patiently during his time in prison.

Part 2: Waiting on God

Think about a situation where you had to wait for something good to happen. Describe the situation, how you felt, and the final outcome:

....

....

Write a short poem or story about the importance of patience, inspired by Joseph's story.

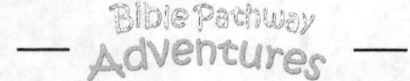

LESSON PLAN - KINDNESS

Healing a paralyzed man: Mark 2:1-12

1. Introduction:

Begin the class by discussing the concept of kindness. Encourage students to share examples of kind acts they have done themselves. Following this discussion, divide them into two teams. Set up a start line and place the 'mystery box' at the finish line. At the start signal, the first player in each team dashes to the box, picks a slip, reads the act of kindness, and dashes back to the start line to act out the act of kindness with the next student in line. Once this student has guessed the act of kindness, they continue the relay. The activity continues until each team member has had a chance to participate. Explain that today's lesson will focus on how the Messiah showed kindness to others, and how we can do the same in our own lives.

** Class prep: prepare for this activity by writing acts of kindness on slips of paper (e.g. helping a friend with homework, giving a compliment). Place these slips in a 'mystery box'.

2. Review key vocabulary:

- **YESHUA:** the Hebrew name for Jesus
- **PARALYZED:** unable to move or walk
- **CAPERNAUM:** a fishing village on the northern shore of the Sea of Galilee
- **SCRIBE:** a teacher of religious law (Torah teacher)
- **SIN:** transgression of the Torah (1 John 3:4)

3. Read Mark 2:1-12 from the Bible, or read the story below:

When Yeshua returned to Capernaum in Galilee, word spread that He was at home. A crowd of people gathered to hear Him teach, and there was no more room, not even at the door. As Yeshua began to teach, four friends came with a paralytic man. Because of the crowd, they could not get near Him. So, they went onto the roof and let him down with his bed through the tiles before Yeshua. When Yeshua saw their faith, He said to the paralytic man, "Your sins are forgiven." Some of the scribes and Pharisees were there and questioned in their hearts, "Why does this man speak like that? This is blasphemy! Who can forgive sins but God alone?" Yeshua knew what they were thinking. "Why do you question these things in your hearts?" He said to them. "Which is easier, to say to the paralytic, 'Your sins are forgiven,' or to say, 'Rise, take up your bed and walk'? But that you may know that the Son of Man has authority on earth to forgive sins." Turning to the paralyzed man, He said, "Rise, pick up your bed, and go home." The paralytic rose, picked up his bed and went home. Everyone was amazed and glorified God, saying, "We have never seen anything like this!"

4. Questions to encourage critical thought:

Contrast: How did the friends' behavior compare to the scribes and Pharisees?
Analyze: Why do you think Yeshua healed the paralyzed man?
Explain: Why do you think the men brought their paralyzed friend to the house?
Describe: How did Yeshua show kindness in this story?

5. Memory verse:

"Whoever pursues righteousness and kindness will find life, righteousness, and honor."
(Proverbs 21:21)

Did you know?

The only Scriptures people had in Bible times was the Old Testament. It included the five books of the Torah, the Prophets, and the Psalms.

6. Activities:

* What's the Word: Kindness in action
* Bible quiz: Healing a paralyzed man
* Bible word search puzzle: Healing a paralyzed man
* Newspaper worksheet: The Capernaum Times
* Map activity: Land of Israel
* Coloring worksheet: Healing a paralyzed man
* Worksheet: Kindness
* Worksheet: God's instructions
* Worksheet: Choose kindness
* Creative writing: Showing kindness
* Coloring page: Proverbs 21:21
* Banner: Kindness

Kindness in action

Read Mark 2:1-12 (ESV). Using the words below,
fill in the blanks to complete the Bible passage.

CAPERNAUM	YESHUA	AMAZED	ROOF
WORD	QUESTION	PARALYZED	FORGIVE

"When Yeshua returned to ………………… after some days, it was reported that He was at home. Many were gathered together so there was no more room, not even at the door. Yeshua preached the ………………… to them. And they came, bringing a paralyzed man carried by four men. When they could not get near Him because of the crowd, they removed the …………………, made an opening, and let down the bed on which the paralyzed man lay. When ………………… saw their faith, He said to the ………………… man, "Son, your sins are forgiven." Some of the scribes were sitting there, questioning in their hearts, "Why does this man speak like that? He is blaspheming! Who can forgive sins but God alone? "Immediately, Yeshua perceived in His spirit that they questioned within themselves, and said, "Why do you ………………… these things in your hearts? Which is easier, to say to the paralyzed man, 'Your sins are forgiven,' or to say, 'Rise, take up your bed and walk'? The Son of Man has authority on earth to ………………… sins." He said to the paralyzed man, "Rise, pick up your bed, and go home." And the man rose, picked up his bed, and went out before them all. They were all ………………… and glorified God, saying, "We never saw anything like this!""

Healing a PARALYZED MAN

Read Mark 2:1-12. Answer the questions below.

1. In which town was Yeshua teaching the people?

2. What happened when people heard Yeshua was home?

3. What was Yeshua doing in Mark 2:2?

4. How many men carried the paralyzed man to Yeshua?

5. Why could these men not get near Yeshua?

6. How did the men get the paralyzed man near Yeshua?

7. What did Yeshua say to the paralytic man when He saw the men's faith?

8. Who questioned Yeshua in their hearts?

9. What did Yeshua say to the paralytic man in Mark 2:11?

10. How did people react to this miracle?

Healing a PARALYZED MAN

Read Mark 2:1-12. Find and circle the words below.

```
K B V G T P Z X C K D J G K X
D E L I A E M J I X N L R I Y
W C Z X B L W I C B U F C N H
A A V Z I Q I R J N E D A D B
H B U P A R A L Y Z E D P N G
Q M R T J K M J E V R W E E B
J R I G H Z Y D T E H Q R S I
C O W R C O S E D I D G N S K
T O L J A F R W Q Z D A A Y B
W F C P H C C I A J M Q U E E
T G N F V O L H T C L Z M S D
J X W Z Z O U E E Y I A Q H I
S O N O F M A N E A J H U U J
K C H N N B J Q R M L P V A S
A R M S C R I B E S U H N D V
```

BED
SCRIBES
MIRACLE
AUTHORITY
PARALYZED
HEAL
CAPERNAUM
KINDNESS
SON OF MAN
GALILEE
YESHUA
ROOF

Sea of Galilee

The Capernaum Times

LAND OF ISRAEL — A DISCIPLESHIP PUBLICATION

Doubting scribes

....

....

....

....

....

Teacher heals paralytic!

....

....

....

....

Fish for sale

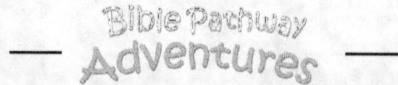

Land of Israel

Peter the disciple lived in the village of Capernaum. He fished on the Sea of Galilee. Find and mark the six places on the map. You may have to use the Internet or an atlas to find the answers. Color the map.

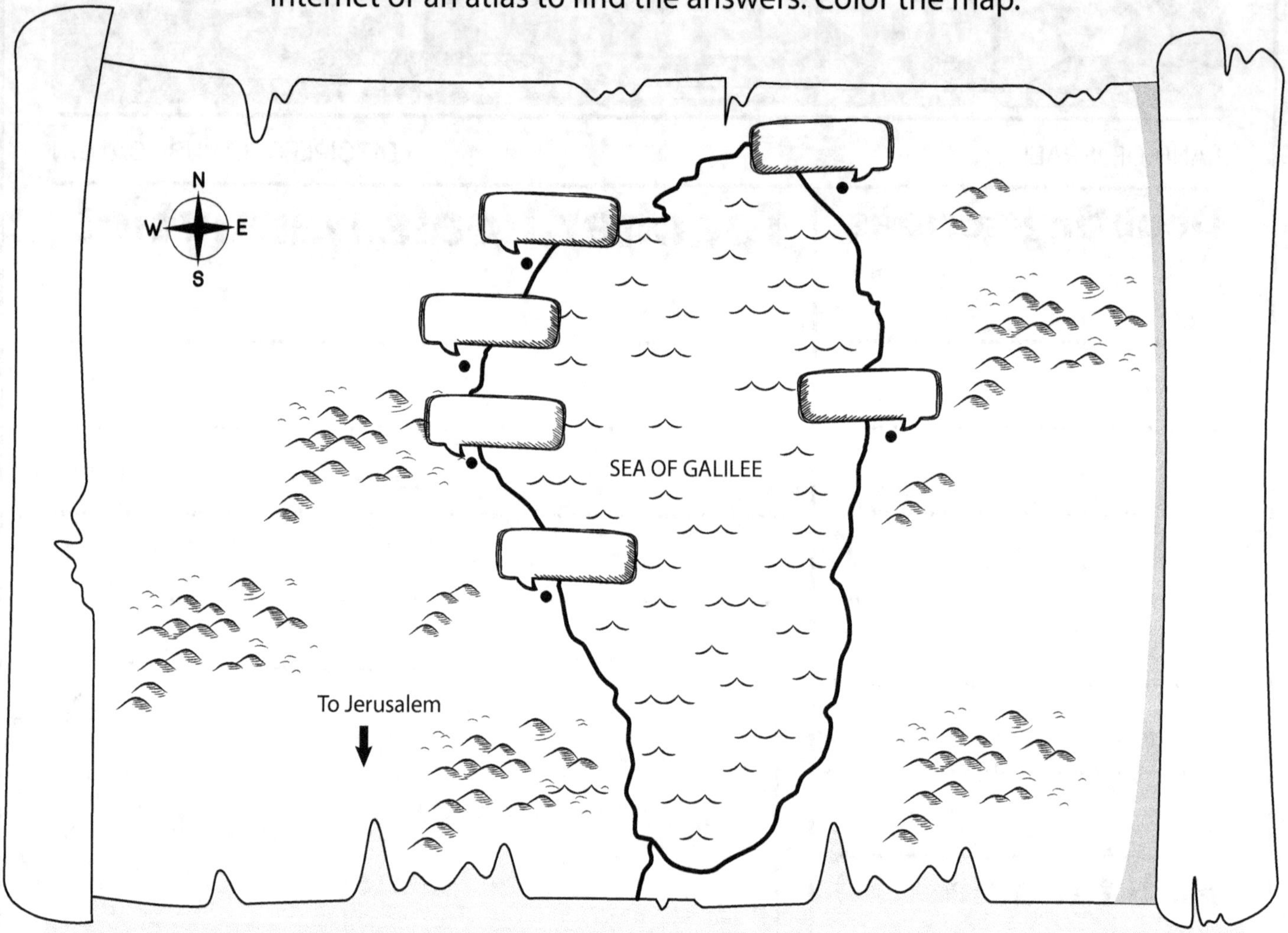

Find and mark these places on the map:

TIBERIAS   KHERSA

BETHSAIDA   MAGDALA

GENNESARET   CAPERNAUM

Healing a paralyzed man

Read Mark 2:5 and write the Bible verse below.

....

....

....

1. Why did the men lower their friend through the roof?

....

....

2. What did Yeshua say to the paralytic man?

....

....

3. What does Yeshua have the authority on earth to do?

....

....

Draw your favorite scene from this story.

The friends showed kindness by…

....

....

Yeshua showed kindness by…

....

....

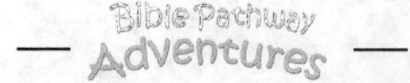

Kindness

God shows us kindness by…

Write about a time you did something kind for a friend.

When someone is unkind to me, I should…

Read 2 Samuel 9:1-13. How did David show God's kindness to Mephibosheth?

God's instructions

Read Proverbs 21:21, Job 6:14, and Micah 6:8. These Bible verses describe the behavior God requires of us, and a promise for those who follow His instructions. Write the Bible verses on the scroll below. Discuss the questions.

1. What does God promise us if we pursue righteousness and kindness?

2. Why do you think kindness is important to God?

3. Read Job 6:14. Why does withholding kindness to a friend show you do not fear God?

Choose kindness

How can you show kindness to others? Write down four actions you could take.

Showing kindness

Read Mark 2:1-12. Complete the activities below.

After reading or listening to Mark 2:1-12, answer these questions:

1. Who showed kindness in this story and how?
   ....

2. How did Yeshua show kindness to the paralyzed man?
   ....

3. How did the man's friends show their faith and kindness?
   ....

Showing kindness:

Kindness is a result of the Holy Spirit working inside you. Write a short paragraph to describe a time you were kind to someone in your family.

....
....
....

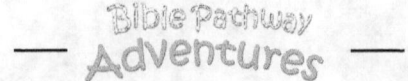

LESSON PLAN - GOODNESS

Josiah and the Torah: 2 Kings 22:1-23:27

1. Introduction:

Begin the class by asking students, "What qualities do you think make a good leader?" Following a class discussion, play the game 'Follow the Leader'. Choose one student to be the leader. The leader will navigate through a series of obstacles or challenges while the rest of the students watch their actions and follow them. The leader's goal is to make wise decisions, demonstrate good leadership qualities, and guide the followers to the destination. Explain that today's lesson will focus on King Josiah, a leader who made good choices that inspired his people to repent (turn back to God's Ways). Throughout this lesson, ask students to consider how they can make wise decisions that are pleasing to God.

2. Review key vocabulary:

- PASSOVER:
  one of God's Appointed Times (Feast)

- JOSIAH:
  king of the Israelites

- HILKIAH:
  the high priest at the temple in Jerusalem

- TORAH:
  first five books of the Bible

- BAAL & ASHERAH:
  false gods of the Canaanites

3. Read 2 Kings 22:1-23:27 from the Bible, or read the story below:

Josiah became king of the Israelites when he was just eight years old. This young king loved God, and followed His commands. As he grew older, he saw that God's temple was in disrepair, and gave Hilkiah, the high priest, money to fix it. During this time, Hilkiah found the Book of the Law (the Torah) that had long been forgotten. Josiah eagerly listened as the Book was read aloud to him. He learned that the Israelites had stopped obeying God, and were actually worshiping false idols. He vowed to set things right. Gathering the Israelites together, he read them the Torah and shared the importance of worshiping the one true God. "It is not good to worship false idols like Baal and Asherah," he cried. After everyone made a covenant before God, Josiah set out to remove every trace of false worship in the land. He destroyed all the altars and idols, leaving nothing behind. Josiah then called upon the people to honor the Passover, an Appointed Time that the Israelites had forgotten. The nation rejoiced as they once again honored God's commands.

4. Questions to encourage critical thought:

Contrast: How did Josiah's young age contrast with his actions as a king?
Analyze: Compare the state of the temple before and after Josiah's efforts.
Explain: Why do you think Josiah tore his clothes when the Torah was read to him?
Describe: How did King Josiah demonstrate goodness in this story?

5. Memory verse:

"For he is good, for his steadfast love endures forever toward Israel." (Ezra 3:11)

Did you know?

Josiah was eight years old when he became the king of Judah (2 Kings 22:1).

6. Activities:

* What's the Word: King Josiah
* Bible quiz: King Josiah
* Bible word search puzzle: Josiah reigns in Judah
* Comprehension worksheet: High Places
* Worksheet: Josiah restores the Passover
* Bible word unscramble: Josiah
* Worksheet: Goodness
* Worksheet: Did You Know?
* Coloring page: Goodness
* Worksheet: I can show Goodness
* Bible activity: Fruit of the spirit sequencing cards
* Banner: Goodness

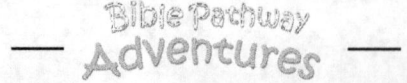

King Josiah

Read 2 Kings 23:3-6 (ESV). Using the words below,
fill in the blanks to complete the Bible passage.

| JOSIAH | JERUSALEM | KIDRON | TEMPLE |
| COMMANDS | JUDAH | PRIESTS | BURNED |

" King .... stood by the column in the temple and made an agreement with God. He promised to follow Him and to obey His ...., the laws, and his rules. He promised to do this with all his heart and soul. He promised to obey the agreement written in this book. All the people stood to show that they promised to follow the agreement. Then the king commanded Hilkiah the high priest, the other priests, and the gatekeepers to bring out of God's .... all the dishes and things that were made to honor Baal, Asherah, and the stars of heaven. Then Josiah burned those things outside .... in the fields in Kidron Valley. Then they carried the ashes to Bethel. The kings of .... had chosen some ordinary men to serve as .... These false priests were burning incense at the high places in every city of Judah and all the towns around Jerusalem. They burned incense to honor Baal, the sun, the moon, the constellations, and all the stars in the sky. But Josiah stopped those false priests. Josiah removed the Asherah pole from God's Temple. He took the Asherah pole outside the city to the .... Valley and burned it there. Then he beat the .... pieces into dust and scattered the dust over the graves of the common people. "

King JOSIAH

Read 2 Kings 22:1-23:28. Answer the questions below.

1. How old was Josiah when he became king?

2. Who was Josiah's father? (2 Kings 21)

3. What materials were purchased to repair the temple in Jerusalem?

4. Who found the Book of the Law?

5. Who read the Book of the Law to Josiah?

6. What did Josiah do when he heard the Book of the Law?

7. What did King Josiah have destroyed?

8. Which meal did Josiah tell the Israelites to observe?

9. What happened after Josiah read the Law to the people?

10. Where did Josiah burn the Asherah pole from the temple?

Josiah reigns IN JUDAH

Read 2 Kings 22:1 - 23:28. Find and circle the words below.

```
H T P Q C W D P P X W E O K R
A C E V Q C W A Q A J X R I G
O L I M D M Q S E Y U E D N Y
V Z T C P X D S T K D H H G T
D Y F A P L B O P U A Z G T J
N R A S R H E V U G H T L X O
K V H Y M S V E G X K W M K S
Z A H U T H H R P D B R O K I
M I C O M M A N D M E N T S A
K S E R V A N T S R J B T B H
F E L O J X T H O S W Y I G S
G O O D N E S S N U N A S E L
B O O K O F T H E L A W P T Q
Y C Q W Y R E P A I R U D D G
H I L K I A H Z P Q D X R I T
```

- PASSOVER
- HILKIAH
- BOOK OF THE LAW
- SERVANTS
- TEMPLE
- COMMANDMENTS
- KING
- ALTARS
- REPAIR
- JUDAH
- JOSIAH
- GOODNESS

High Places

In the Bible, "High Places" refer to a location, usually on a mountain or hill, often dedicated to the worship of false gods. Shrines could include an altar and a sacred object, such as a stone pillar or wooden poles. In 2 Kings 23, King Josiah defiled the High Places so the Israelites could not worship false idols there. However, not all High Places were set apart for idol worship.

The earliest mention of a worship site, later called a High Place, is found in Genesis 12:6–8 where Abram built altars to God at Shechem and Hebron. He later built an altar in the region of Moriah in obedience to God's command to sacrifice his son, Isaac. Jacob set up a stone pillar at Bethel (Genesis 28:18–19), and Mount Sinai is a notable High Place where Moses received the ten commandments from God. Despite God's warnings, the Israelites continued to worship false gods like Molech, and built High Places for Baal (Jeremiah 32:35). Although King Solomon built God's temple in Jerusalem, he created High Places near the city for his many wives to worship their false gods.

1. What is a High Place?

2. Name three Bible characters who built altars in High Places.

Color the altar!

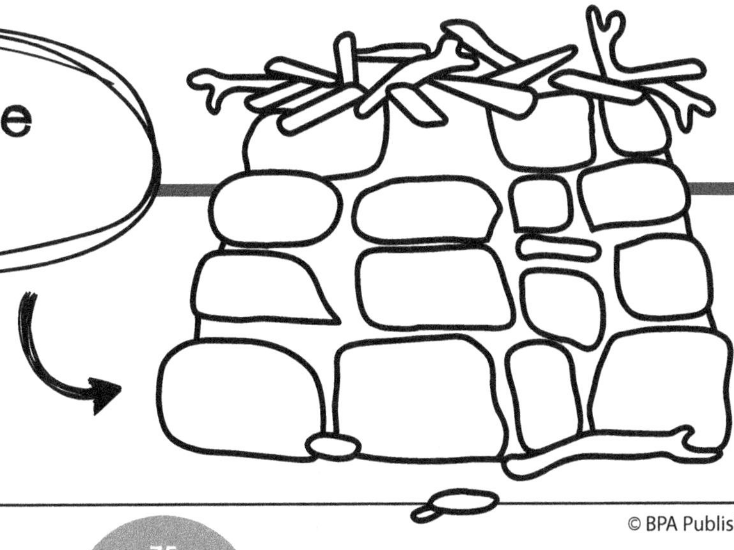

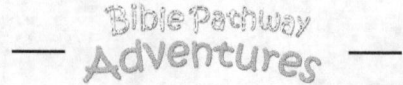

Josiah restores the Passover

"King Josiah commanded all the people, 'Keep the Passover, as it is written in this Book of the Covenant.' For no such Passover had been kept since the days of the judges who judged Israel, or during all the days of the kings of Israel or Judah. But in the eighteenth year of King Josiah this Passover was kept in Jerusalem. Moreover, Josiah put away the mediums and the necromancers and the household gods and the idols and all the abominations that were seen in the land of Judah and in Jerusalem, that he might establish the words of the law that were written in the book that Hilkiah the priest found in the house of the Lord. Before him there was no king like him, who turned to God with all his heart and with all his soul and with all his might, according to all the Law of Moses, nor did any like him arise after him."
(2 Kings 23:21-25)

Read Exodus 12 and Deuteronomy 28:1-14. How did God instruct the Israelites to honor the Passover and Feast of Unleavened Bread? If people obey God's commandments, what blessings are promised?

King Josiah restored the Passover. He brought goodness back into the land. Unscramble the words to learn more about King Josiah's repentance.

ovssaPre .... hgih cepals ....

ralemeusJ .... eeltmp ....

urbdne htoarsci .... oBok fo hte alw ....

dsepedo rpesist .... klhiaiH ....

✸ Read about Josiah's repentance in 1 Kings 22-23 (ESV).

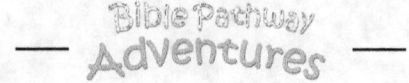

Goodness

I show goodness to my family by…

Read Jeremiah 6:16. What are the ancient paths that are good?

King Josiah pleased God by…

Draw a picture of God's commandments.

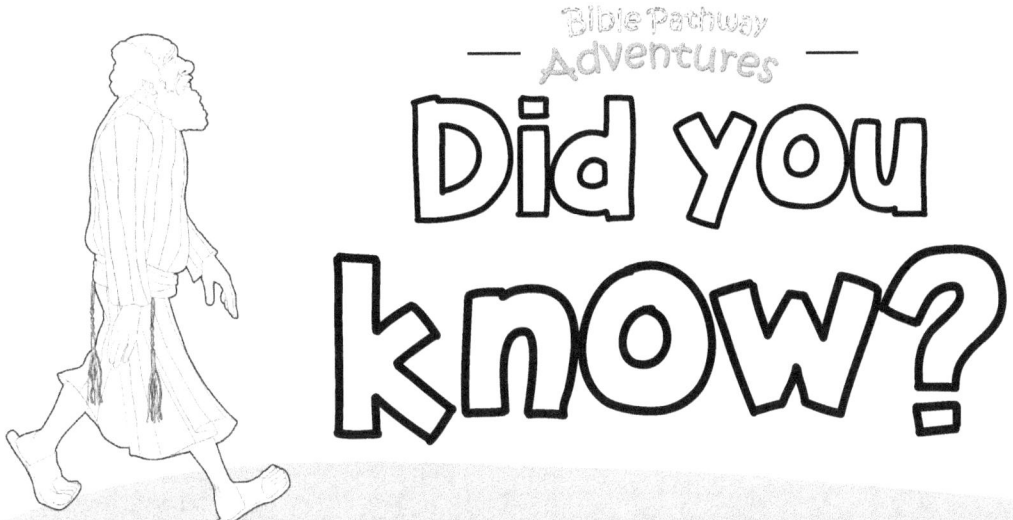

Did you know?

While the Israelites journeyed through the wilderness for forty years, God gave them instructions to obey. He compared them to a young wife raised up for the purpose of honoring God, who is Israel's husband by covenant. However, when the Israelites reached the Promised Land, they began disobeying His instructions, and did not honor His Ways. Rather than remaining faithful, they played the "harlot" by following the ungodly practices of their neighbors, such as the Canaanites. The same rituals and customs the pagans used to worship their false gods, the Israelites used to worship the God of Abraham, Isaac and Jacob. God compared these practices to a disloyal wife committing adultery against her husband, and described this behavior as spiritual unfaithfulness (spiritual adultery). Have you ever wondered why God was unhappy with the Israelites in 2 Kings 22-23? They were worshipping other gods. Goodness had gone from the land.

Read 2 Kings 23:1-25. Draw your favorite scene from this Bible passage.

For He is good, for His steadfast love endures forever towards Israel.

Ezra 3:11

I can show goodness...

Read Galatians 6:10. God asks us to do good to all people, especially to people who believe in Him. Write a paragraph to describe a time you were good to someone. What did you do?

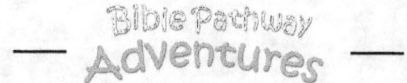

LESSON PLAN - FAITHFULNESS

The faithful servant: Genesis 12:1-7, 18:1-19, and 21:1-5

1. Introduction:

Begin the class by asking students, "One day, you hear a voice telling you to pack your bags, leave your home, and travel to a place you've never seen. Would you go?" After a class discussion, divide students into teams, set up an obstacle course, and mark the 'Promised Land' at the end. Blindfold the first student on each team at the starting line. On "go", they must navigate the course based on verbal directions from their teammates. After reaching the Promised Land, they return to the starting line and pass the blindfold to the next teammate. The first team to get all members to the Promised Land and back wins the game. Explain that today's lesson will focus on Abraham, a faithful servant who listened to God's instructions, and did what He said.

2. Review key vocabulary:

- **ABRAM / ABRAHAM:** Hebrew patriarch, father of Isaac and grandfather of Jacob
- **SARAI / SARAH:** Abraham's wife
- **LAND OF CANAAN:** the land where Abraham and his family settled
- **ISAAC:** Abraham and Sarah's son
- **FAITHFUL:** to remain loyal and steadfast

3. Read Genesis 12:1-7, 18:1-19, & 21:1-5 from the Bible, or read the story below:

A man named Abram lived peacefully with his wife, Sarai, and his nephew, Lot in a foreign land. One day, God asked him to leave his home and move to another land far away – the land of Canaan. "Go from your country to the land that I will show you. I will make of you a great nation," said God. With faith as his compass, Abram followed God's instructions and left Haran with his family and all their possessions. When they arrived in the land of Canaan, God affirmed His promise to Abram - this land would belong to his future generations, turning Abram's descendants into a great nation. As the years passed, Abram and Sarai (renamed by God as Abraham and Sarah), grew old. One afternoon, they were visited by three strangers. These strangers brought an amazing message - Sarah, despite her old age, would have a son. Sarah laughed to herself, saying, "I am worn out, and my husband is old." But the strangers told her that nothing was impossible for God. Finally, the day came when Sarah held her baby boy – Isaac - in her arms. And Abraham, at the age of 100, had become a father again. God had indeed blessed his faithful servant!

4. Questions to encourage critical thought:

Contrast: How did Abraham's reaction to God's instructions in Genesis 12:1-7 differ from Sarah's reaction to the news of her future son in Genesis 18:1-19?
Analyze: What challenges do you think Abraham faced on the way to the land of Canaan?
Explain: Why do you think Sarah laughed when strangers told her that she would have a baby?
Describe: How did Abraham show God that He was a faithful servant?

5. Memory verse:

"God is the faithful God. He keeps His covenant of love to a thousand generations of those who love Him and keep His commandments..." (Deuteronomy 7:9)

Did you know?

Abraham was 100 years old when his son Isaac was born (Genesis 21:5).

6. Activities:

* What's the Word: A faithful servant
* Bible quiz: Abraham
* Bible word search puzzle: Abraham's faithfulness
* Bible activity: Abraham's journey
* Map activity: Footsteps of Abraham
* Coloring worksheet: The call of Abram
* Worksheet: Faithfulness
* Worksheet: Interview Abraham!
* Coloring page: Faithfulness
* Creative writing: Faithfulness rewarded
* Banner: Faithfulness

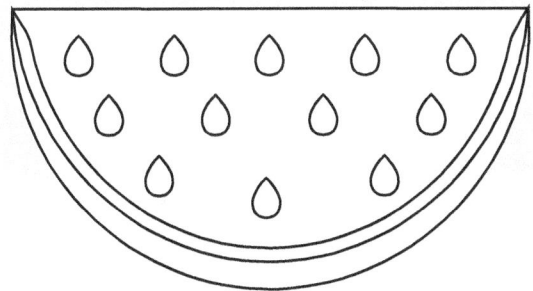

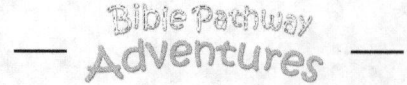

A faithful servant

Read Acts 7:2-8 (ESV). Using the words below,
fill in the blanks to complete the Bible passage.

| ABRAHAM | COVENANT | CHALDEANS | WORSHIP |
| PROMISED | ISRAEL | FATHER | TWELVE |

"God appeared to .... while he was still in Mesopotamia, before he lived in Harran. 'Leave your country and your people,' God said, 'and go to the land I will show you. So Abraham left the land of the .... and settled in Harran. After the death of his .... Terah, God sent him to the land of Canaan. He gave him no inheritance, not even enough ground to set his foot on. But God .... Abraham that he and his descendants would possess the land, even though at that time Abraham had no child. God spoke to him in this way: 'For four hundred years your descendants (the Israelites) will be strangers in a foreign country where they become slaves. But I will punish that nation,' God said, 'and afterward they will come out of that country and .... Me in this place.' Then He gave Abraham the .... of circumcision. And Abraham became the father of Isaac and circumcized him eight days after his birth. Later, Isaac became the father of Jacob, and Jacob became the father of the .... tribes of ...."

Read Genesis 12:1-20, 14:1-15:20, 17:1-27, and 21:1-34. Answer the questions below.

1. Where was Abram born?

2. Who was Abram's father?

3. Who did Abram marry?

4. Which land did God promise to Abram?

5. What did Abram do after Lot was taken prisoner?

6. What did Melchizedek give to Abram?

7. What did God's new name for Abraham mean?

8. How old was Abraham when he became a father?

9. What was the name of Abraham's special son?

10. Abraham traveled to which land to escape the famine?

Abraham's FAITHFULNESS

Read Genesis 12 and 21. Find and circle each of the words from the list below.

```
F C S M D N E F C S P G C H H
B G P U X T A I O A K K O A L
X L F J A M Y I V R D D F R A
P T E X O P P R E A Z B F A N
A A U S D O F W N I X L S N D
K M V H S Q Y V A M R F P U O
Z P R O M I S E N L S C R C F
H P T N W I N S T D X G I E C
K R K Q Y Y K G D L I B N I A
W F C M L K W U Z K U L G S N
J O U R N E Y X L S U W B A A
U L G R E A T N A T I O N A A
Q B T N I M G C R U Q R N C N
U P I X L U A B R A H A M J C
G H F A I T H F U L N E S S B
```

PROMISE

GREAT NATION

FAITHFULNESS

ABRAHAM

BLESSING

OFFSPRING

JOURNEY

HARAN

COVENANT

ISAAC

SARAI

LAND OF CANAAN

Abraham's journey

Read Genesis 12. Abraham left his home and traveled to the land of Canaan. What do you think he took with him? Think about life in ancient Mesopotamia and make a list of items. Draw each item inside the sack.

1. ....
2. ....
3. ....
4. ....
5. ....
6. ....
7. ....
8. ....
9. ....
10. ....

www.biblepathwayadventures.com
Fruit of the Spirit Activity Book

© BPA Publishing Ltd 2023

Footsteps of Abraham

Read Genesis 12. Abraham left the city of Ur and traveled to the land of Canaan. From Ur, he traveled 700 miles to the borders of modern-day Iraq, another 700 miles into Syria, and then onto the land of Canaan. Do you think this journey is possible today? Why / why not? Trace Abraham's journey by connecting the dots. Color the map.

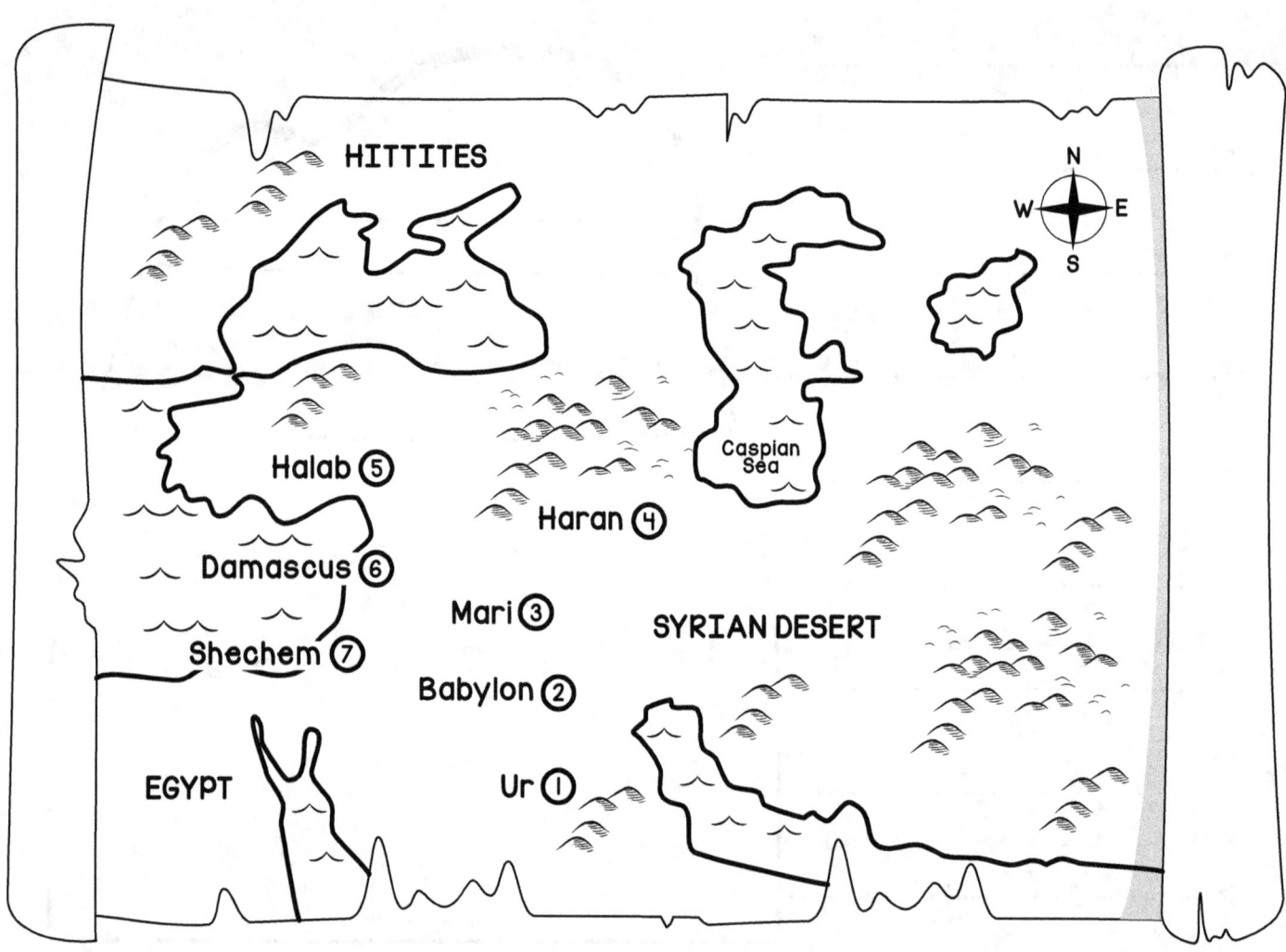

The call of Abram

Read Genesis 12:1-20. Write a short summary of this story.

....

....

....

1. What did God tell Abram to do?
....
....

2. Who traveled with Abram to the land of Canaan?
....
....

3. Why did Sarai and Abram go to the land of Egypt?
....
....

Draw your favorite scene from this story.

What could the life of Abram teach me?

....
....

God used Abram to…

....
....

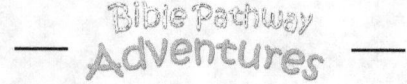

Faithfulness

Read Psalm 37:28-29. God will reward my faithfulness by…

....
....
....
....
....
....
....
....

Read Hebrews 11:8-12. Abraham showed God he was faithful by…

....
....
....
....
....
....
....
....
....
....

Faithfulness is difficult when…

....
....
....
....
....

If the story of Abraham was a book, the cover would look like this…

Interview Abraham!

God said to Abraham, "Look at the sky and count the stars if you can. This is how many descendants you will have." (Genesis 15:5) Imagine you are Abraham. A magazine has sent you a questionnaire. Tell them about God's promise, and why you believe He is faithful.

1. Introduce yourself.

....
....

2. Tell us about God's promise to you.

....
....

3. Describe your journey to the land of Canaan.

....
....

4. Why do you believe God is faithful?

....
....

"By faith Abraham obeyed when he was called to go out to the place which he would receive as an inheritance."

(Hebrews 11:8)

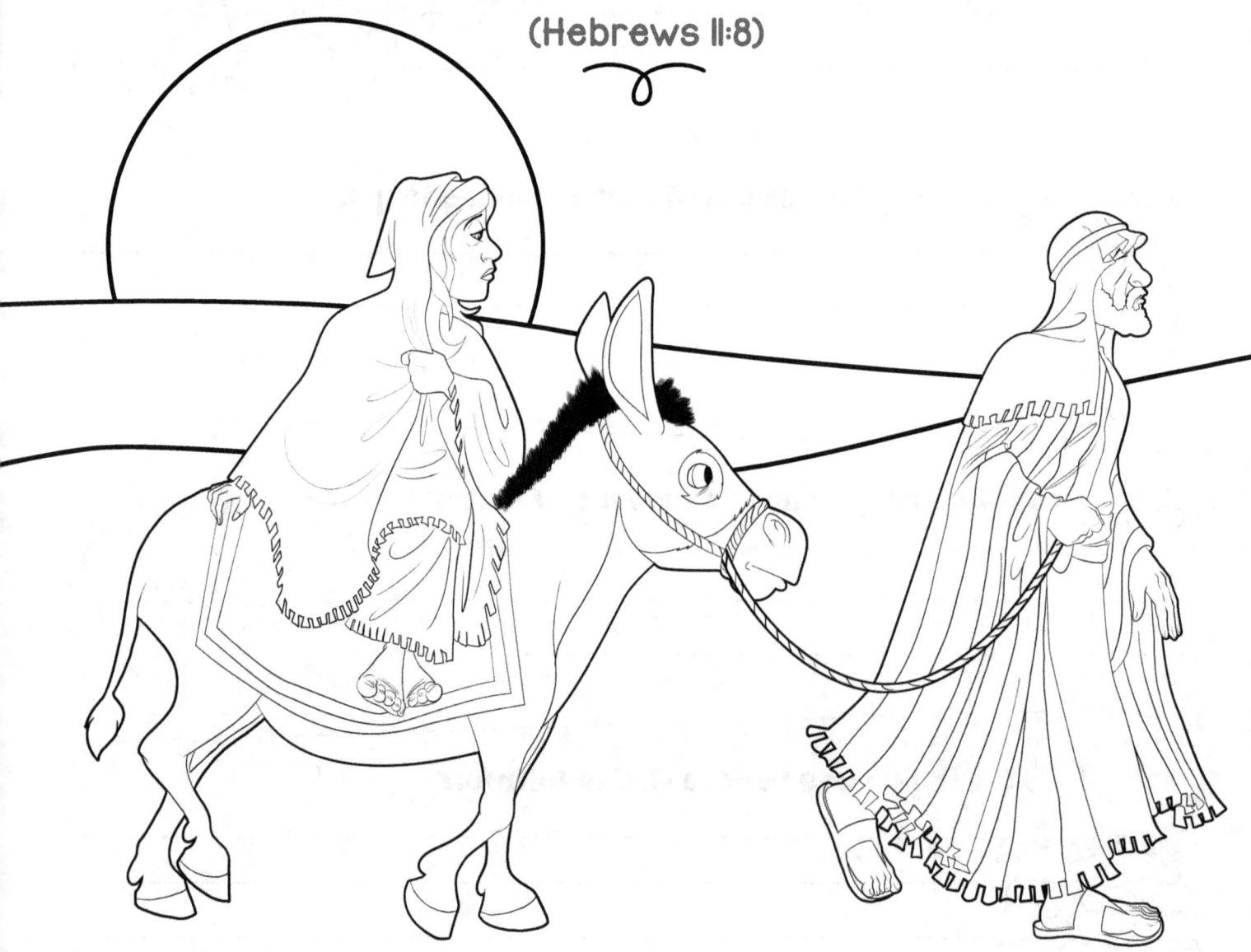

Faithfulness rewarded

Read Hebrews 11:8-19. Abraham followed God's instructions and traveled to the land of Canaan. God rewarded Abraham's faithfulness by making his descendants as numerous as the stars in the sky. Write a paragraph to explain how you are faithful to God.

LESSON PLAN - GENTLENESS

Miriam and Aaron oppose Moses: Numbers 12:1-16

1. Introduction:

Begin the class by discussing the concept of gentleness (strength under control). After a class discussion, divide students into teams and play 'Feather Relay Race' to introduce the concept of gentleness. Each team gets a feather and a spoon. The first person in each team must place the feather on the spoon and walk as quickly as they can to the finish line and back without the feather falling off. If the feather falls, they must stop and place it back on the spoon before they continue. Explain that today's lesson will focus on Moses and how he dealt with his brother and sister in the wilderness. He did not try to defend himself. Instead, he was gentle towards them and let God take care of the situation.

2. Review key vocabulary:

- **TABERNACLE:** the 'tent of meeting' for the Israelites in the wilderness

- **MOSES:** leader of the Israelites

- **LEPROSY:** a skin disease

- **SERVANT:** a person who performs duties for others, a person who serves others

- **PROPHET:** a person who speaks what God wants them to say

3. Read Numbers 12:1-16 from the Bible, or read the story below:

Miriam and Aaron, Moses' sister and brother, spoke against him because he had married a woman from Cush. "Has God spoken only to Moses? Hasn't he also spoken to us?" they grumbled. Now Moses was a gentle man (humble, meek), more than anyone else on earth. God heard Miriam and Aaron's complaints and called the three of them to the tabernacle. There He appeared in a pillar of cloud, and said to Miriam and Aaron, "If there is a prophet among you, I will make Myself known to him in a vision, and speak to him in a dream. But I speak to Moses directly, plainly and without riddles. Why did you speak against My faithful servant?" His anger flared and He departed. As the cloud left, Miriam was struck with leprosy and her skin turned as white as snow. Aaron pleaded with Moses not to hold their foolishness against them. And Moses, who was worried about his sister, begged God to heal her. But God said, "If her father had spit in her face, shouldn't she be ashamed for seven days? Put her outside the camp for seven days. After that, she shall be brought in."

4. Questions to encourage critical thought:

Contrast: How do you think Miriam's behavior changed towards Moses before and after God struck her with leprosy?
Analyze: Why did Miriam and Aaron criticize Moses?
Explain: Why do you think God punished Miriam with leprosy and not Aaron, even though they both spoke against Moses?
Describe: How did Moses demonstrate gentleness (strength under control) in this story?

5. Memory verse:

"A gentle answer turns away wrath, but a harsh word stirs up anger." (Proverbs 15:1)

Did you know?

Moses was eighty years old when he appeared before Pharaoh and led the Israelites out of Egypt (Exodus 7:7).

6. Activities:

* What's the Word: Opposing authority
* Bible quiz: Miriam and Aaron oppose Moses
* Bible word search: The gentle leader
* Worksheet: Who was Moses?
* Worksheet: The tabernacle
* Worksheet: My travel diary
* Coloring worksheet: Be gentle…
* Worksheet: Moses
* Coloring page: Fruit of the Spirit
* Worksheet: The power of gentleness
* Banner: Gentleness
* Bible craft: Make a fruit of the spirit lapbook

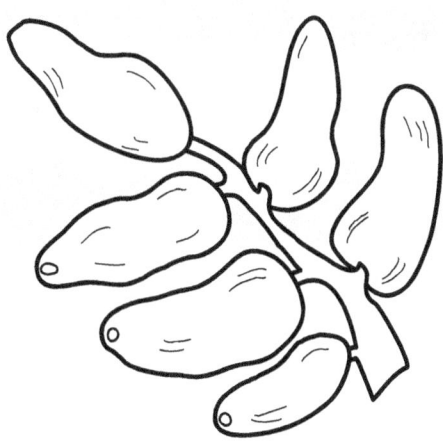

Opposing authority

Read Numbers 12:1-9 (WEB). Using the words below, fill in the blanks to complete the Bible passage.

| AARON | TENT | HOUSE | SERVANT | ANGER |
| CUSHITE | YAHWEH | DREAM | FAITHFUL | PILLAR |

" Miriam and .... spoke against Moses because of the Cushite woman whom he had married; for he had married a .... woman. They said, "Has .... indeed spoken only with Moses? Hasn't he spoken also with us?" And Yahweh heard it. Now the man Moses was very humble, more than all the men who were on the surface of the earth. Yahweh spoke suddenly to Moses, to Aaron, and to Miriam, "You three come out to the .... of Meeting!" The three of them came out. Yahweh came down in a .... of cloud, and stood at the door of the Tent, and called Aaron and Miriam; and they both came forward. He said, "Now hear my words. If there is a prophet among you, I, Yahweh, will make myself known to him in a vision. I will speak with him in a .... My .... Moses is not so. He is .... in all my .... With him, I will speak mouth to mouth, even plainly, and not in riddles; and he shall see Yahweh's form. Why then were you not afraid to speak against my servant, against Moses?" Yahweh's .... burned against them; and He departed. "

Aaron and Miriam OPPOSE MOSES

Read Numbers 12:1-15. Answer the questions below.

1. What relation were Aaron and Miriam to Moses?

2. Why did Aaron and Miriam speak against Moses?

3. Moses was more gentle (meek/humble) than whom?

4. Where did God ask Moses, Aaron, and Miriam to assemble?

5. How did God appear to Moses, Aaron, and Miriam?

6. How did God speak to Moses?

7. What happened to Miriam after God left?

8. What did Moses ask God to do?

9. How did God react to Moses prayer?

10. How long was Miriam outside the camp?

The gentle LEADER

Moses was both gentle and strong. Read Numbers 12:1-15. Find and circle each of the words from the list below.

MEEKNESS

MIRIAM

HUMBLE

CUSHITE

MOSES

AARON

WILDERNESS

TABERNACLE

GENTLENESS

SERVANT

HOUSE OF ISRAEL

PILLAR OF CLOUD

Who was Moses?

Read Exodus 2-3, 12-20, and Numbers 12, 20. Complete the worksheet below.

God told Moses to:

....

Describe Moses' leadership style in the wilderness:

....

....

Moses showed gentleness by…

....

Moses is most famous for:

....

....

Five words that describe Moses:

1. ....

2. ....

3. ....

4. ....

5. ....

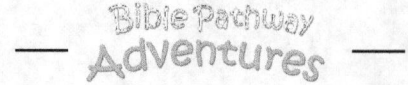

The tabernacle

The tabernacle was a sacred place where God met the Israelites during the forty years they lived in the desert. It represented His throne on the earth and symbolized His dwelling among His people. It was here the Israelites came together to worship Yah and offer sacrifices. The tabernacle was a tent-like structure covered by animal skins surrounded by a white linen fence. The tabernacle itself was divided into two places – the Holy Place and the Holy of Holies – and only the priests could enter these areas. All the furniture in the Holy Place was made of gold, just as God instructed.

It was the job of the Levites to carry the tabernacle and set it up wherever the Israelites pitched camp. When the Levites erected the tabernacle, they placed it in the center of the camp. Moses, Aaron, and the priests camped on the east side next to the entrance, and the other tribes of Israel were grouped into four camps around the tabernacle's outer fence.

Read Exodus 26:1-31:18. Answer the questions below.

1. What was the purpose of the tabernacle?
2. Which two men were put in charge of building the tabernacle?
3. What oil was used to keep the lamps burning in the tabernacle?
4. What was the purpose of the brazen altar?
5. Where was the mercy seat located?

My travel diary

Moses led the Israelites through the desert for forty years. Imagine you are an Israelite. What did you see on your way to the Promised Land? Record your journey below.

I learned...

I Heard...

God showed me...

The strangest thing I saw was...

I found...

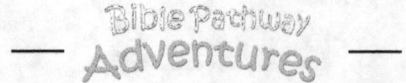

Be gentle...

Read Colossians 3:12 and write the Bible verse below.

....

....

....

Write about a time in your life where you showed gentleness.

....
....
....
....
....
....
....
....
....

Read Proverbs 15:1. Draw the proverb so your friends will guess it.

What is the meaning of Colossians 3:12?

....

....

Colossians 3:12 teaches me...

....

....

Moses

Think about Moses' life. How did God teach Moses gentleness?

....
....
....
....
....
....
....

Read Numbers 12:3-16. God intervened on Moses' behalf by…

....
....
....
....
....
....
....
....
....
....

Titus 3:1-2 tell us to…

....
....
....
....
....
....

If the story of Moses' life was a book, the cover would look like this…

"The Fruit of the Spirit is love, joy, peace, patience, kindness, goodness, faithfulness, gentleness and self-control..."

(Galatians 5:22-23)

The power of gentleness

Read Numbers 12:1-16. Answer the questions and complete the activities below.

Why did Miriam and Aaron oppose Moses?

....

What did God declare about Moses' authority?

....

How did God respond to Miriam's actions?

....

What happened to Miriam, and how was she healed?

....

Activities:

1. Think of a situation in your life, such as helping a friend or being patient with someone, where you can display gentleness. Write a paragraph describing how you can demonstrate gentleness in this situation.

2. Read the story of Miriam and Aaron opposing Moses. Consider the concept of gentleness, and then draw a scene from this story. Write a paragraph explaining how your scene shows gentleness. Remember: Gentleness is a fruit of the Spirit that involves strength, humbleness and self-control in our words and actions.

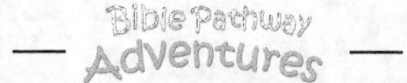

LESSON PLAN - SELF-CONTROL

David spares Saul's life: 1 Samuel 24:1-22

1. Introduction:

Begin the class by asking students, "Have you ever found yourself in a situation where you had to make a difficult decision or control your actions?" Following a class discussion, play a game called 'Red Light, Green Light' to introduce the concept of self-control. One student will be a 'traffic light' while everyone else forms a line. The traffic light stands a distance away, facing away from the players. When the traffic light says "green light", everyone can move forward. But as soon as the traffic light says "red light", all players must freeze and stop moving. If anyone is caught moving during a red light, they go back to the starting line. The game continues until someone tags the traffic light, becoming the new traffic light for the next round. Explain that today's lesson will focus on David and how he demonstrated self-control in the story of David spares Saul's life.

2. Review key vocabulary:

- **DAVID:** an Israelite, the next king of Israel
- **KING SAUL:** king of the Israelites
- **ENGEDI:** a desert oasis on the edge of the Judean desert
- **PHILISTINES:** an ancient people who lived on the south coast of Canaan
- **ISRAELITES:** members of the 12 tribes of Israel

3. Read 1 Samuel 24:1-22 from the Bible, or read the story below:

After chasing the Philistines, King Saul heard that David was hiding in the wilderness of Engedi. He took 3000 men and went to find him. On the way, he needed to use the bathroom and went into a cave where David and his men were hiding. David's men said to him, "This is the day God spoke of when He said, 'Behold, I will give your enemy into your hand!'" David crept up to Saul and cut off a piece of his robe. Afterwards, he felt guilty for harming Saul. He said to his men, "I cannot hurt God's anointed one. Do not attack him." And so, Saul safely left the cave. A short time later, David came out of the cave and called to Saul, saying, "Why do you listen to others who want to harm me? Today, God gave you into my hands, but I spared you. I won't harm you, even though you want to kill me." Saul answered, "You are more righteous than me. You have repaid me good, whereas I have repaid you evil. God will reward you for your kindness. Promise me you won't hurt my family when you become king." Then Saul returned home while David and his men went on their way.

4. Questions to encourage critical thought:

Contrast: How did David's actions compare to his men's thoughts?
Analyze: Why do you think David's conscience troubled him after cutting off a piece of Saul's robe?
Explain: Why did David refuse to hurt Saul, even though Saul wanted to kill him?
Describe: How did David demonstrate self-control in this story?

5. Memory verse:

"A fool gives full vent to his anger but a wise man keeps himself under control."
(Proverbs 29:11)

Did you know?

When David was a young man, King Saul had him play the harp to take away his depression (1 Samuel 16:22-23).

6. Activities:

* What's the Word: Mercy in the wilderness
* Bible quiz: David spares Saul's life
* Bible word search: David spares Saul's life
* Coloring worksheet: David's test of self-control
* Comprehension worksheet: Who was King Saul?
* Worksheet: Self-control
* Bible verse puzzle: Do you have self-control?
* Worksheet: Self-control superheroes!
* Coloring page: Self-control
* Worksheet: I can show self-control
* Bible craft: Guess the Bible verse
* Banner: Self-control

Mercy in the wilderness

Read 1 Samuel 24:1-7 (ESV). Using the words below,
fill in the blanks to complete the Bible passage.

| PHILISTINES | DAVID | ROBE | MEN |
| GOD | CAVE | ANOINTED | ISRAEL |

"When Saul returned from following the ...., he was told, "Behold, David is in the wilderness of Engedi." Saul took three thousand chosen men out of all .... and went to find .... and his men in front of the Wild goats' Rocks. He came to the sheepfolds where there was a ...., and went in to relieve himself. Now David and his men were sitting in the innermost parts of the cave. And David's men said to him, "Here is the day of which .... said to you, 'Behold, I will give your enemy into your hand, and you shall do to him as it shall seem good to you.'" Then David arose and stealthily cut off a corner of Saul's .... But afterwards, David's heart struck him because he had cut off a corner of Saul's robe. He said to his men, "God forbid that I should do this thing to my lord, who is God's ...., to put my hand against him, seeing he is God's anointed." David persuaded his .... with these words and did not permit them to attack Saul. And Saul left the cave and went on his way."

David spares SAUL'S LIFE

Read 1 Samuel 24:1-22. Answer the questions below.

1. Where had Saul returned from?
2. How many men did Saul choose to help him find David?
3. Why did Saul go into the cave?
4. In what part of the cave were David and his men sitting?
5. What did David do to Saul inside the cave?
6. What did David forbid his men to do?
7. What did David do when Saul saw him outside the cave?
8. What did Saul do after David had finished speaking?
9. What kingdom did Saul say would be established in David's hand?
10. Where did Saul and David go after they had finished speaking?

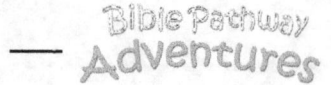

David spares SAUL'S LIFE

Read 1 Samuel 24:1-22. Find and circle the words below.

```
H E B R E W O C Z W R I Z C C
S V T A S S E L S M O S N D S
E S U U H E Y G C U B R H R X
L E O J L F N H O D E A K E A
F O X L O H U H N R X E U N L
C I T P D H T Y V O G L U G M
O W F H O I U J M C I I Z E D
N K E X Q H E Y W K R T G D A
T V C I G J I R F P Z E F I V
R R O D I P T N K V Y T X G I
O M D K I N G D O M G G E Q D
L M W Z F L W T D K Y M R I B
H I L Q R X A P Y Z B I X Y P
J A G S K I N G S A U L P W J
A N O I N T E D H N L C V G J
```

HEBREW

KINGDOM

ROCK

ENGEDI

TASSELS

SOLDIER

ISRAELITE

ANOINTED

ROBE

KING SAUL

SELF-CONTROL

DAVID

David's test of self-control

Read 1 Samuel 24:1-22. Write a summary of this Bible story below.

....

....

....

1. Where did David find Saul?

....

....

2. What did David do to Saul?

....

....

3. Why did David tell his men not to attack Saul?

....

....

Draw your favorite scene from this story.

David showed self-control by…

....

....

This story teaches me…

....

....

Who was King Saul?

Saul, a Benjaminite from the mountain village of Gibeah, was Israel's first king. Saul's kingdom was very small by today's standards; it only included the territory of Benjamin and the central highlands of Israel. King Saul created a base in the town of Gibeah, a royal administration, and a proper army. Even though Saul's new kingdom wasn't large or powerful, it laid the foundation for David's future military and economic success.

At the beginning of King Saul's reign, his army defeated the Ammonites, Moabites, Edomites, and Amalekites. However, God didn't favor King Saul for very long. After Saul disobeyed God by saving King Agag of the Amalekites along with some of their best cattle, God rejected him and chose David as the next king of Israel. Saul became very jealous of David and spent years trying to kill him.

1. How big was King Saul's kingdom?

2. Why do you think King Saul became jealous of David?

Color King Saul!

Self-control

Read Luke 4:13. How did Yeshua resist temptation?

....
....
....
....
....
....
....
....

Read Proverbs 29:20. What does it mean to speak in haste?

....
....
....
....
....
....
....
....
....
....

Read Nehemiah 4. Nehemiah showed God he was self-controlled by…

....
....
....
....
....

If the story of David & Saul was a book, the cover would look like this…

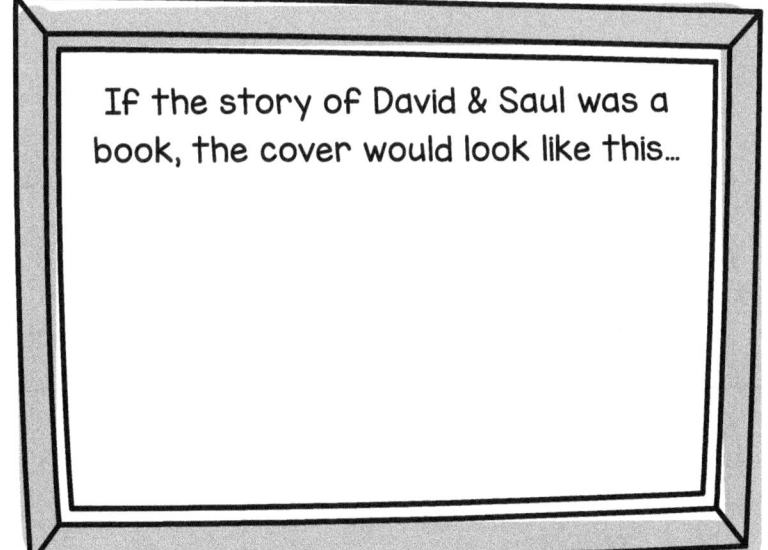

Do you have self-control?

What does the Bible say about a man with no self-control? This Bible verse is written in code. Use the chart at the bottom of the page to fill in the missing letters and crack the code! *Hint: Read Proverbs 25:28 (ESV)*

$\underset{1}{A}\ \underset{14}{M}\ \underset{1}{A}\ \underset{11}{N}\ \underset{23}{W}\ \underset{21}{I}\ \underset{26}{T}\ \underset{5}{H}\ \underset{2}{O}\ \underset{24}{U}\ \underset{26}{T}\ \underset{13}{S}\ \underset{6}{E}\ \underset{10}{L}\ \underset{25}{F}\ -\ \underset{22}{C}\ \underset{2}{O}\ \underset{11}{N}\ \underset{26}{T}\ \underset{12}{R}\ \underset{2}{O}\ \underset{10}{L}$

$\underset{21}{I}\ \underset{13}{S}\ \underset{10}{L}\ \underset{21}{I}\ \underset{4}{K}\ \underset{6}{E}\ \underset{1}{A}\ \underset{22}{C}\ \underset{21}{I}\ \underset{26}{T}\ \underset{18}{Y}\ \underset{15}{B}\ \underset{12}{R}\ \underset{2}{O}\ \underset{4}{K}\ \underset{6}{E}\ \underset{11}{N}\ \underset{21}{I}\ \underset{11}{N}\ \underset{26}{T}\ \underset{2}{O}$

$\underset{1}{A}\ \underset{11}{N}\ \underset{9}{D}\ \underset{10}{L}\ \underset{6}{E}\ \underset{25}{F}\ \underset{26}{T}\ \underset{23}{W}\ \underset{21}{I}\ \underset{26}{T}\ \underset{5}{H}\ \underset{2}{O}\ \underset{24}{U}\ \underset{26}{T}\ \underset{23}{W}\ \underset{1}{A}\ \underset{10}{L}\ \underset{10}{L}\ \underset{13}{S}$

A	B	C	D	E	F	G	H	I	J	K	L	M
1	15											

N	O	P	Q	R	S	T	U	V	W	X	Y	Z
	2											

Self-control superheroes!

Self-control means making wise choices and controlling our actions, even in challenging situations. Just like David, let's have self-control in our own lives. Read 1 Samuel 24:1-22. Complete the worksheet below.

1. The cave encounter:

Draw a picture of King Saul and David in the cave.

2. Questions:

Why did David's men think it was the perfect opportunity to harm Saul?

Why did David feel guilty after cutting off a piece of Saul's robe?

Why did David choose not to harm Saul, even though Saul wanted to kill him?

How did Saul respond to David's mercy and kindness?

3. Practising self-control:

How did other famous Bible heroes demonstrate self-control? Next to each name, write an example of how they showed self-control in different situations.

Joseph: ....

Daniel: ....

Esther: ....

Yeshua: ....

Paul: ....

"For God gave us a Spirit not of fear but of power and love and self-control."

(2 Timothy 1:7)

I can show self-control

Read Titus 2:1-12. Write a short paragraph to explain why God wants you to have self-control. Why is it important to show self-control?

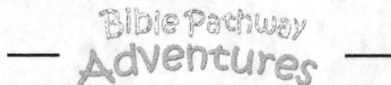

Make a hanging mobile

You will need:
1. Card stock
2. Paint, felt pens, or crayons
3. String
4. Glue stick or tape
5. Wooden sticks

Instructions:

1. Ask your child to color the piece of fruit inside each circle.
2. When your child has finished drawing, cut out the mobile pieces and glue onto heavy card stock. Wait for the glue to dry.
3. Carefully cut out the mobile pieces.
4. Make a hole at the top of each mobile piece, string the pieces together, and attach to a piece of wood.

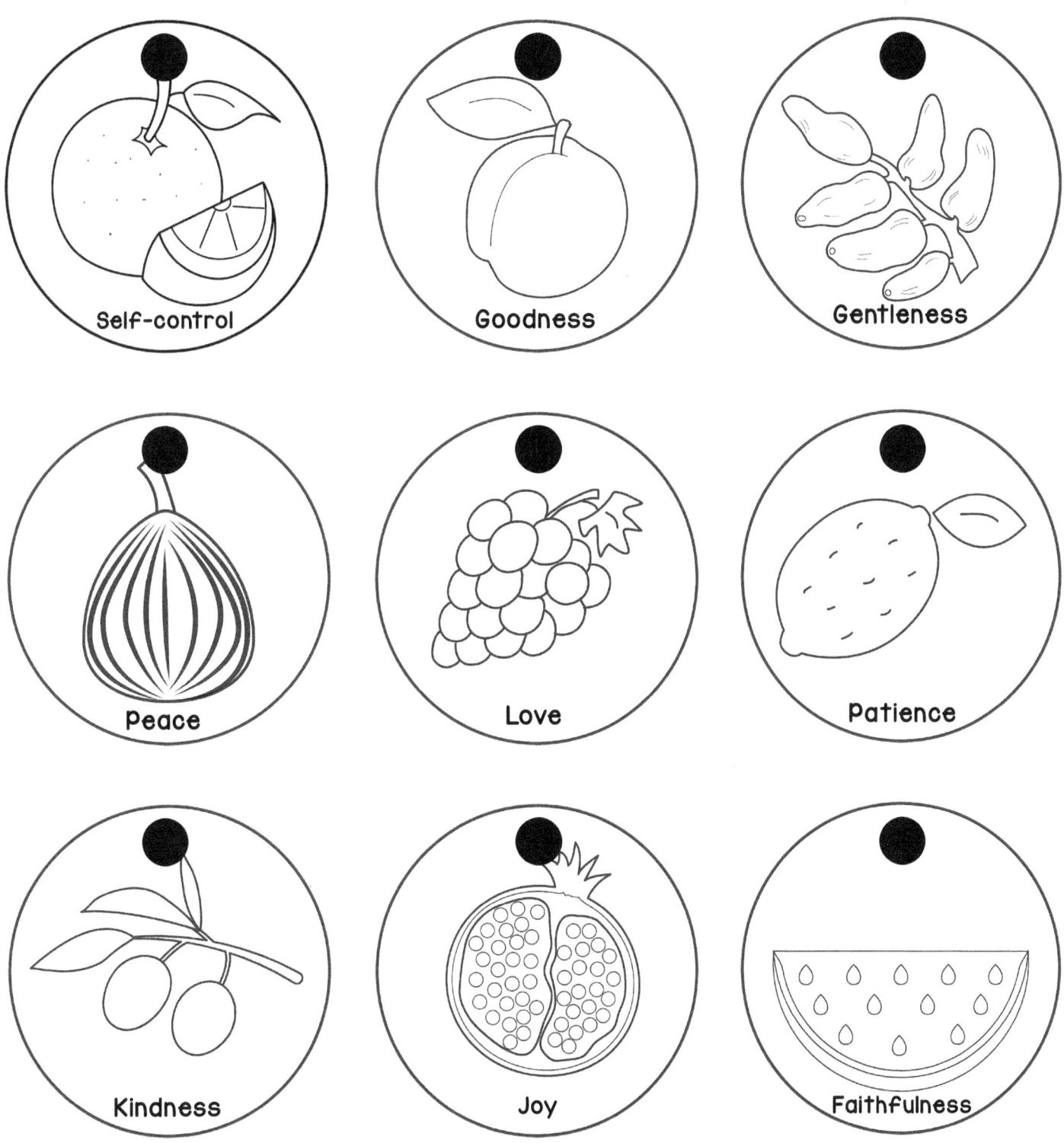

Fruit of the Spirit puppets

You will need:
1. Heavy card stock
2. Paint, felt pens, or crayons
3. School glue or glue sticks, and tape

Instructions:

1. Color each puppet.
2. Paste the puppet sheets onto a piece of heavy card stock and wait for the glue to dry.
3. Carefully cut out each of the puppets.
4. Wrap the tabs of each puppet around your finger and tape.

Make a door hanger

You will need:
1. Heavy card stock or construction paper
2. Paint, felt pens, or crayons
3. Extra-strength glue sticks or tape

Instructions:

1. Copy or print out the door hanger templates and paste onto heavy card stock. Wait for the glue to dry and then cut out each template.
2. Color and cut out the fruit circles. Paste the fruit circles onto the door hangers. Write the name of a Fruit of the Spirit beside each circle.
3. Make a reversible door hanger by pasting two templates together, back-to-back.
4. Laminate or seal each door hanger using clear laminating sheets.

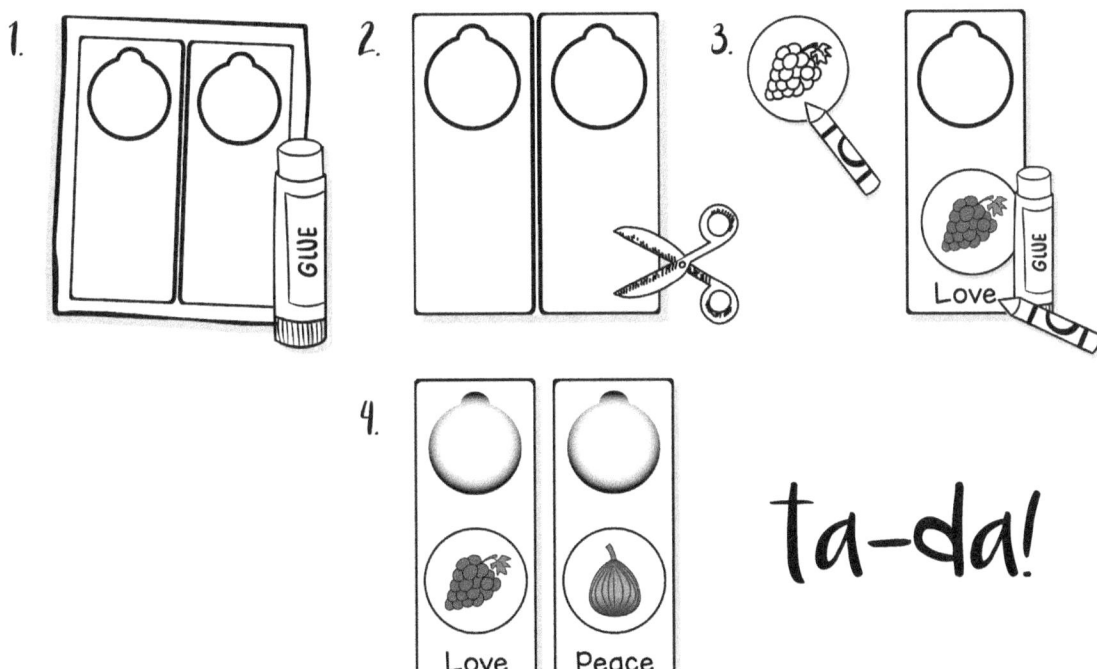

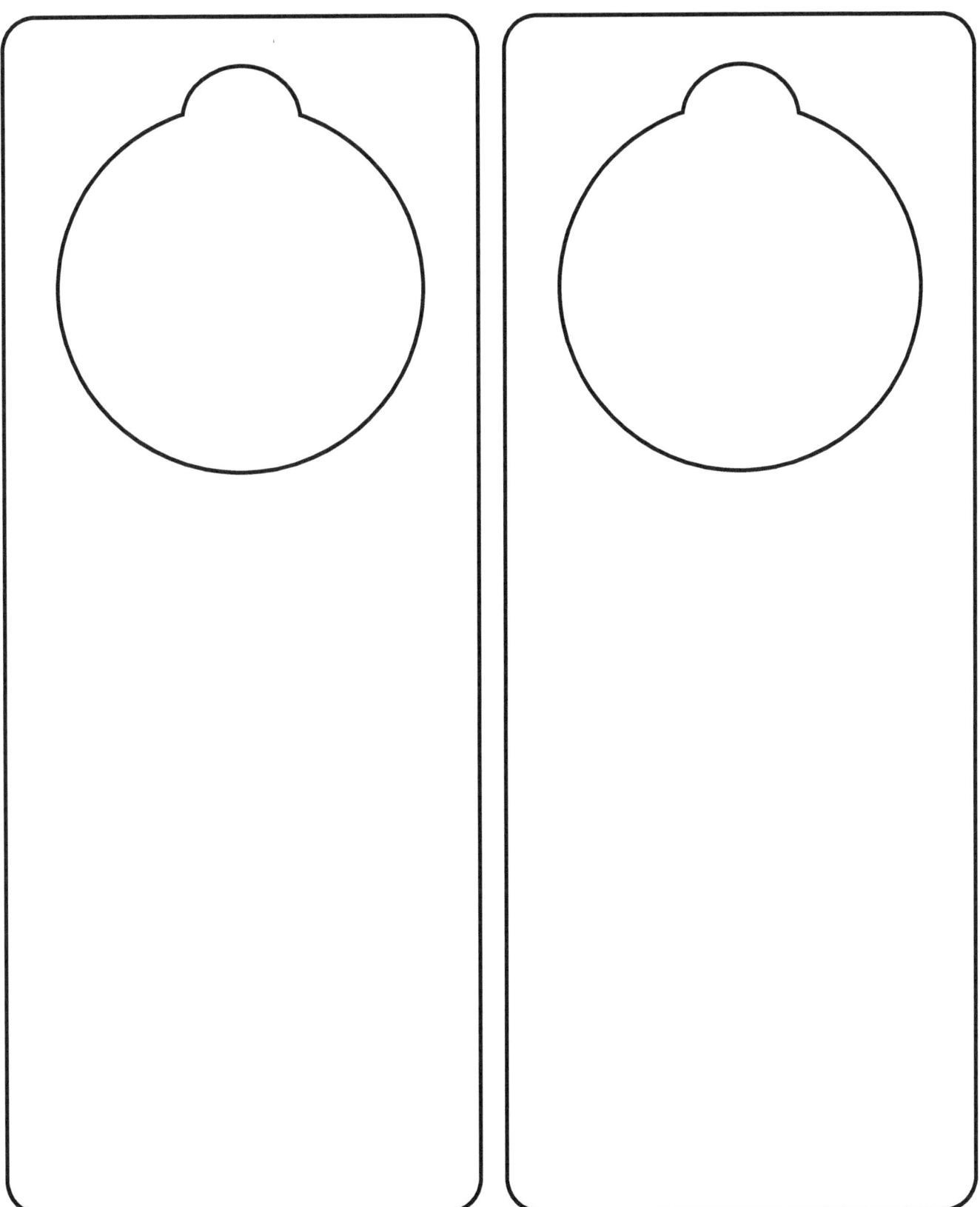

Make a fruit basket

You will need:

1. Two thick foam or paper plates (use the sturdy kind with a "lip")
2. Heavy card stock
3. Brown paint or crayons
4. Fruit of the Spirit template (see following pages)
5. Extra-strength glue sticks or School glue

Instructions:

1. Cut one of the paper plates in half. Use the concave side for the front of the fruit basket.
2. Make a handle by cutting another paper plate in half and leaving a handle around the edge. Glue the two sides together. Paint or color the paper plates brown.
3. While the paper plate is drying, color the fruit. Write a fruit of the Spirit on the back of each piece of fruit.
4. Place the fruit in the basket. Use this fruit to help children remember the fruits of the Spirit.

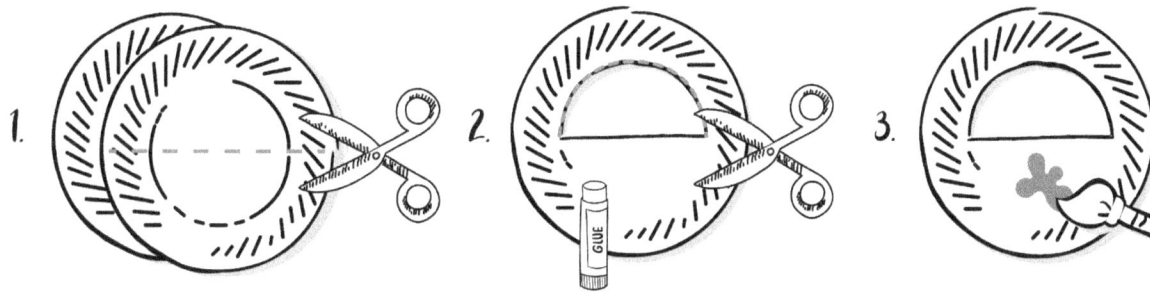

ta-da!

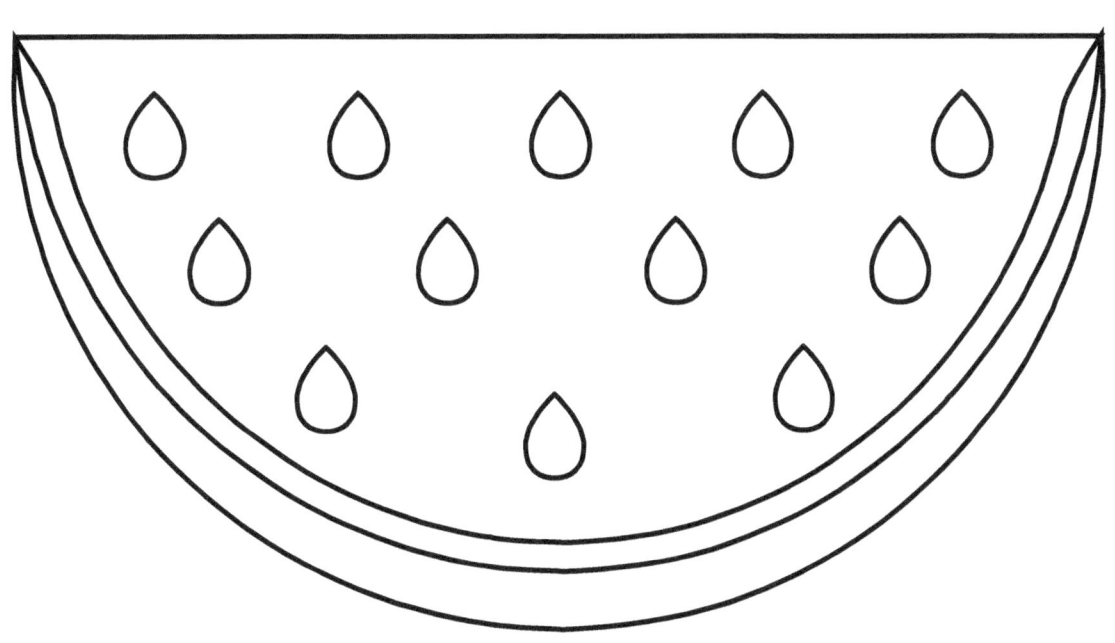

Sequencing cards

Read Galatians 5:22-23. Cut out the cards and place them in the correct order.

JOY

KINDNESS

SELF-CONTROL

FAITHFULNESS

LOVE

PEACE

GENTLENESS

GOODNESS

PATIENCE

FRUIT OF THE SPIRIT

Make your own lapbook

You will need:

1. An 8" x 10" file folder
2. Fruit of the Spirit mini-booklets (see next pages)
3. Paint, felt pens, or crayons
4. Extra-strength glue sticks or tape

Instructions:

1. Use one 8" x 10" file folder.
2. Open and flatten the folder.
3. Find the center of the right side of the folder and fold lengthwise along the center line on the right side.
4. Find the center of the left side of the folder and fold lengthwise along the center line on the left side. Both sides should meet in the middle.
5. Hand each child a copy of the fruit of the spirit templates (see following pages) and ask them to cut out and make nine mini-booklets. Inside each mini-booklet, write a Bible verse that matches that fruit of the spirit. Refer to the Answer Key for suggested Bible verses.
6. Ask the children to paste the booklets into their lapbooks.

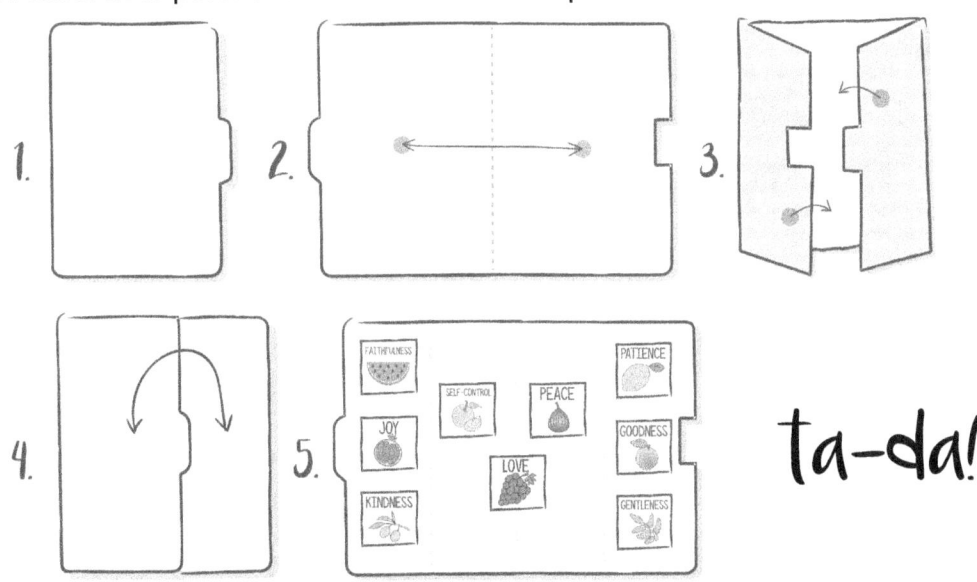

	FAITHFULNESS
	JOY
	KINDNESS

	SELF-CONTROL
	LOVE
	PEACE

	PATIENCE
	GOODNESS
	GENTLENESS

Guess the Bible verse

You will need:
1. Heavy card stock
2. Pens or felt pens
3. Extra-strength glue sticks or tape

Instructions:

1. Choose a Bible verse and then print out the same number of fig templates as words in the Bible verse.
2. Carefully cut out each fig piece.
3. Fold up the bottom of the piece so that it is in front of the picture of the fig.
4. Write one word of the Bible verse on the bottom of each fig piece.
5. Place the fig pieces in a row. Have your students throw a ball at each fig piece to reveal a word. Continue the game until all the fig pieces have been knocked over and students can read the Bible verse.

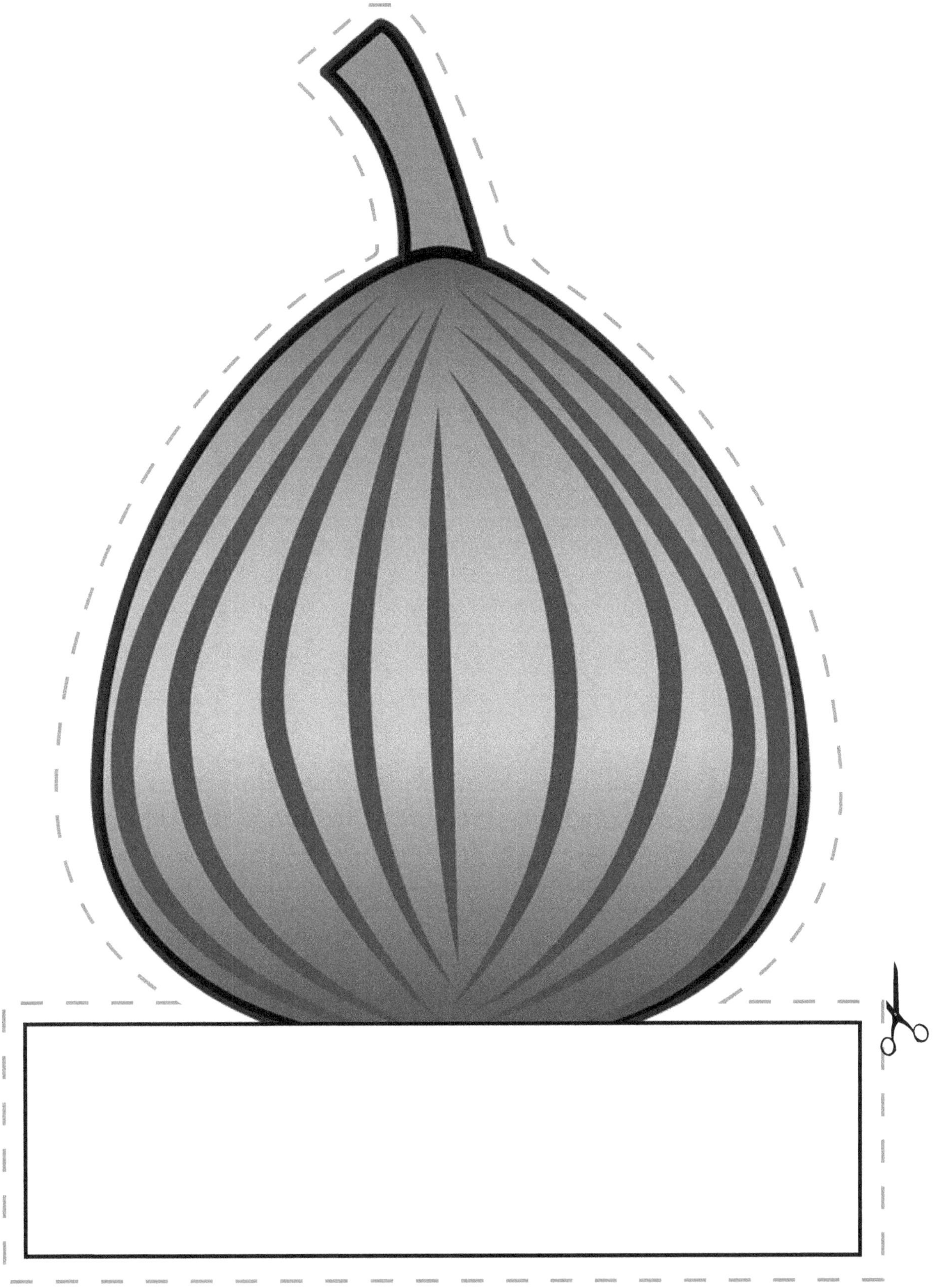

ANSWER KEY

Lesson One: Love
What's the Word: A lesson in love
The Torah teacher, desiring to justify himself said to Yeshua, "Who is my neighbor?" Yeshua replied, "A man was going down from Jerusalem to Jericho and fell among robbers, who stripped him, beat him and departed, leaving him half dead. Now by chance a priest was going down that road, and when he saw him he passed by on the other side. Likewise, a Levite when he came to the place and saw him, passed by on the other side. But a Samaritan, as he journeyed, came to where he was and when he saw him, he had compassion. He bound up his wounds, pouring on oil and wine. Then he set him on his own animal and brought him to an inn and took care of him. The next day he took out two denarii and gave them to the innkeeper, saying, 'Take care of him, and whatever more you spend I will repay you when I come back.' Which of these three do you think proved to be a neighbor to the man who fell among the robbers?" He said, "The one who showed him mercy." And Yeshua said to him, "Go and do likewise."

Bible quiz: The good Samaritan
1. A Torah teacher (lawyer)
2. "You shall love God with all your heart, soul, and strength; and your neighbor as yourself." (Deuteronomy 6:5)
3. To Jericho
4. He was robbed and beaten
5. A priest
6. A Levite
7. A Samaritan
8. Cleaned his wounds and paid an innkeeper to take care of him
9. Two denarii
10. "He who showed mercy on him."

Bible word search: The good Samaritan

Coloring worksheet: The good Samaritan
1. Jericho
2. He was robbed and beaten
3. Cleaned the traveler's wounds and paid an innkeeper to take care of him

Lesson Two: Joy
What's the Word: Earthquake!
About midnight Paul and Silas were praying and singing hymns to God, and the prisoners were listening. Suddenly there was a great earthquake and the foundations of the prison were shaken. Immediately all the doors opened and everyone's chains were unfastened. When the jailer woke and saw that the prison doors were open, he drew his sword and was about to kill himself, thinking that the prisoners had escaped. But Paul cried with a loud voice, "Do not harm yourself, for we are all here." The jailer called for lights and rushed in. Trembling with fear, he fell down before Paul and Silas. "What must I do to be saved?" And they said, "Believe in Yeshua the Messiah and you will be saved, you and your household." They spoke the word of God to him and to all who were in his house. And the jailer took them and washed their wounds; and he was baptized at once, he and all his family. Then he took them into his house and gave them food. And he rejoiced along with his entire household that he had believed in God.

Bible quiz: Paul & Silas in prison
1. Philippi
2. The stocks
3. Prayed and sang songs to God
4. An earthquake
5. He thought the prisoners had escaped
6. To wash their wounds and hear the Word of God
7. Because they believed in God
8. They learned that Paul was a Roman citizen
9. Apologized to Paul and asked him to leave the city
10. Lydia

Bible word search: Paul & Silas in prison

Map activity: The Roman Empire
1. Europe, Africa, Asia
2. Portugal, England, Spain, Italy, France, Switzerland, Egypt, Israel, Turkey, Syria, Greece, Spain, Belgium

Bible word scramble: Why did the jailer rejoice?
And he rejoiced along with his entire household that he had believed in God.

Lesson Three: Peace
What's the Word: Surviving the den…
The king commanded and Daniel was brought and cast into the den of lions. The king declared to Daniel, "May your God whom you serve continually, deliver you!" And a stone was brought and laid on the mouth of the den, and the king sealed it with his own signet ring and with the signet ring of his lords, that nothing might be changed concerning Daniel. Then the king went to his palace and spent the night fasting and did not sleep. The next morning, the king hurried to the den of lions. As he came near the den where Daniel was imprisoned, he cried out in anguish, "O Daniel, servant of the living God, has your God, whom you serve continually, been able to deliver you from the lions?" Then Daniel said to the king, "O king, live forever! My God sent his angel and shut the lions' mouths, and they have not harmed me, because I was found blameless before him; and also before you, O king, I have done no harm." Then the king was exceedingly glad, and commanded that Daniel be taken up out of the den. Daniel was taken up out of the den and no harm was found on him because he had trusted in God.

Bible quiz: Daniel and the lions
1. Darius
2. Make him a high official over the whole kingdom
3. Because Daniel was faithful and no fault was found in him
4. A group of Magi
5. Daniel was thrown into the lions' den
6. For praying to Yahweh, the god of Abraham, Isaac and Jacob
7. Darius
8. With a large stone
9. An angel of God shut the lion's mouths
10. Because Daniel trusted God

Bible word search: Daniel and the lions

Worksheet: Finding peace in tough times
a) The king made a law that for 30 days anyone who prayed to any god or human being except to him, King Darius, would be thrown into the lions' den
b) Daniel continued to pray to God three times a day, just as he had always done, even though he knew about the law
c) Daniel was arrested and thrown into the lions' den because he did not obey the new law
d) Daniel was unharmed in the lions' den because of his faith. God sent an angel to close the mouths of the lions, and the next morning, he was found to be without any harm. The king then praised Daniel's God and proclaimed His greatness throughout the kingdom

Bible verse puzzle: Who has great peace?
"Great peace have those who love your law; nothing can make them stumble." (Psalm 119:165 ESV)

Lesson Four: Patience
What's the Word: Joseph rises to power
Pharaoh said to his servants, "Where can we find a man like this who has the Spirit of God?" Then Pharaoh said to Joseph, "Since God has shown you all this, there is none so discerning and wise as you are. You shall be over my house and all my people shall order themselves as you command. Only as regards the throne will I be greater than you." And Pharaoh said to Joseph, "I have set you over all the land of Egypt." He took his signet ring from his hand and put it on Joseph's hand, clothed him in fine linen, and put a gold chain about his neck. And he made him ride in his second chariot. And they called

out before him, "Bow the knee!" Thus Pharaoh set him over all the land of Egypt. Then Pharaoh said to Joseph, "I am Pharaoh and without your consent no one shall lift up hand or foot in the land of Egypt." And Pharaoh called Joseph's name Zaphenath-paneah and gave him in marriage to Asenath, the daughter of Potiphera, priest of On. So Joseph went out over the land of Egypt. He was thirty years old when he entered the service of Pharaoh, king of Egypt.

Bible quiz: Joseph
1. Potiphar threw Joseph in prison
2. The prison warden chose Joseph to take care of all the prisoners
3. Pharaoh had his chief cupbearer and baker thrown in prison
4. Pharaoh held a feast for his servants
5. The chief cupbearer
6. Joseph explained Pharaoh's dreams
7. Pharaoh gave Joseph his ring, linen clothes, a gold chain and a wife
8. Joseph was 30 years old
9. Joseph married Asenath, the daughter of Potiphera priest of On
10. This story took place in the land of Egypt

Bible word search: Joseph in Egypt

Coloring worksheet: Joseph's patience
1. Pharaoh ruled over the land of Egypt
2. Joseph explained Pharaoh's dreams and showed wisdom
3. A special ring, fine linen robe, a gold chain, and a wife

Comprehension worksheet: Ancient Egyptian dreams
1. The Egyptians used their dreams to cure illnesses, make important decisions, and even to decide where to build a temple or when to fight a battle
2. The Egyptians were so interested in the meaning of their dreams, they even had temples like the Temple of Horus in Edfu, where they would lie in 'dream beds' and hope to have a dream about advice, comfort or healing
3. Common images included breaking stones, teeth falling out, drowning in the Nile, drinking warm beer, and eating white bread. A dream book was discovered in the village of Deir el-Medina, near the Valley of the Kings. It contained a list of dreams describing activities such as pounding, brewing, weaving, sightseeing, stirring, and plastering

Coloring activity: Fruit of the Spirit
"But the fruit of the Spirit is love, joy, peace, patience, kindness, goodness, faithfulness, gentleness, self-control; against such things there is no law." (Galatians 5:22-23)

Lesson Five: Kindness
What's the Word: Kindness in action
When Yeshua returned to Capernaum after some days, it was reported that He was at home. Many were gathered together so there was no more room, not even at the door. Yeshua preached the Word to them. And they came, bringing a paralyzed man carried by four men. When they could not get near Him because of the crowd, they removed the roof, made an opening, and let down the bed on which the paralyzed man lay. When Yeshua saw their faith, He said to the paralyzed man, "Son, your sins are forgiven." Some of the scribes were sitting there, questioning in their hearts, "Why does this man speak like that? He is blaspheming! Who can forgive sins but God alone?" Immediately, Yeshua perceived in His spirit that they questioned within themselves, and said, "Why do you question these things in your hearts? Which is easier, to say to the paralyzed man, 'Your sins are forgiven,' or to say, 'Rise, take up your bed and walk'? The Son of Man has authority on earth to forgive sins." He said to the paralyzed man, "Rise, pick up your bed, and go home." And the man rose, picked up his bed, and went out before them all. They were all amazed and glorified God, saying, "We never saw anything like this!"

Bible quiz: Healing a paralyzed man
1. Capernaum
2. So many gathered that there was no more room in the house
3. Teaching the Word (Scriptures)
4. Four men
5. Because the house where Yeshua was teaching was too crowded
6. Made an opening in the roof and lowered the paralyzed man down to Him
7. "Son, your sins are forgiven."
8. The scribes
9. "I say to you, rise, pick up your bed, and go home."
10. They were all amazed and glorified God, saying, "We never saw anything like this!"

Bible word search: Healing a paralyzed man

Coloring worksheet: Healing a paralyzed man
1. The men lowered their friend through the roof because there was no room in the house or doorway
2. Yeshua said to the paralytic man, "Son, your sins are forgiven."
3. Yeshua has the authority to forgive sin

Lesson Six: Goodness
What's the Word: King Josiah
King Josiah stood by the column in the temple and made an agreement with God. He promised to follow Him and to obey His commands, the laws, and his rules. He promised to do this with all his heart and soul. He promised to obey the agreement written in this book. All the people stood to show that they promised to follow the agreement. Then the king commanded Hilkiah the high priest, the other priests, and the gatekeepers to bring out of God's Temple all the dishes and things that were made to honor Baal, Asherah, and the stars of heaven. Then Josiah burned those things outside Jerusalem in the fields in Kidron Valley. Then they carried the ashes to Bethel. The kings of Judah had chosen some ordinary men to serve as priests. These false priests were burning incense at the high places in every city of Judah and all the towns around Jerusalem. They burned incense to honor Baal, the sun, the moon, the constellations, and all the stars in the sky. But Josiah stopped those false priests. Josiah removed the Asherah pole from God's Temple. He took the Asherah pole outside the city to the Kidron Valley and burned it there. Then he beat the burned pieces into dust and scattered the dust over the graves of the common people.

Bible quiz: King Josiah
1. Eight years old
2. Amon
3. Timber and stone
4. Hilkiah the High Priest
5. Shaphan

6. He tore his clothes
7. Incense altars, altars of the Baals, and Asherah poles
8. The Passover meal
9. The people joined in the covenant
10. At the brook Kidron

Bible word search: Josiah reigns in Judah

Comprehension worksheet: High Places
1. A High Place was a raised piece of ground or an altar on low land, such as a valley. Shrines often included an altar and a sacred object such as a stone pillar or wooden pole in various shapes
2. Abram (Abraham), Jacob, and Solomon

Worksheet: Josiah restores the Passover
1. This month is to be for you the first month, the first month of your year. Tell the whole community of Israel that on the tenth day of this month each man is to take a lamb for his family, one for each household. The animals you choose must be year-old males without defect, and you may take them from the sheep or the goats. Take care of them until the fourteenth day of the month, when all the members of the community of Israel must slaughter them at twilight. Then they are to take some of the blood and put it on the sides and tops of the doorframes of the houses where they eat the lambs. That same night they are to eat the meat roasted over the fire, along with bitter herbs, and bread made without yeast. This is how you are to eat it: with your cloak tucked into your belt, your sandals on your feet and your staff in your hand. Eat it in haste; it is God's Passover. This is a day you are to commemorate for the generations to come you shall celebrate it as a festival to God —a lasting ordinance. For seven days you are to eat bread made without yeast. On the first day remove the yeast from your houses, for whoever eats anything with yeast in it from the first day through the seventh must be cut off from Israel. On the first day hold a sacred assembly, and another one on the seventh day. Do no work at all on these days,

except to prepare food for everyone to eat; that is all you may do. Celebrate this day as a lasting ordinance for the generations to come. In the first month you are to eat bread made without yeast, from the evening of the fourteenth day until the evening of the twenty-first day. For seven days no yeast is to be found in your houses. And anyone, whether foreigner or native-born, who eats anything with yeast in it must be cut off from the community of Israel. Eat nothing made with yeast. Wherever you live, you must eat unleavened bread.

2. If you faithfully obey the voice of God, being careful to do all his commandments that I command you today, God will set you high above all the nations of the earth. And all these blessings shall come upon you and overtake you, if you obey the voice of God. Blessed shall you be in the city, and blessed shall you be in the field. Blessed shall be the fruit of your womb and the fruit of your ground and the fruit of your cattle, the increase of your herds and the young of your flock. Blessed shall be your basket and your kneading bowl. Blessed shall you be when you come in, and blessed shall you be when you go out. God will cause your enemies who rise against you to be defeated before you. They shall come out against you one way and flee before you seven ways. God will command the blessing on you in your barns and in all that you undertake. And he will bless you in the land that God is giving you. God will establish you as a people holy (set apart) to himself, as he has sworn to you, if you keep the commandments of God and walk in his ways. And all the peoples of the earth shall see that you are called by the name of God, and they shall be afraid of you. And God will make you abound in prosperity, in the fruit of your womb and in the fruit of your livestock and in the fruit of your ground, within the land that God swore to your fathers to give you. God will open to you his good treasury, the heavens, to give the rain to your land in its season and to bless all the work of your hands. And you shall lend to many nations, but you shall not borrow. God will make you the head and not the tail, and you shall only go up and not down, if you obey the commandments of God, which I command you today, being careful to do them, and if you do not turn aside from any of the words that I command you today, to the right hand or to the left, to go after other gods to serve them.

Bible word unscramble: Josiah
Passover, Jerusalem, burned chariots, deposed priests, high places, temple, Book of the law, Hilkiah

Lesson Seven: Faithfulness
What's the Word: A faithful servant
God appeared to Abraham while he was still in Mesopotamia, before he lived in Harran. 'Leave your country and your people,' Yahweh said, 'and go to the land I will show you. So Abraham left the land of the Chaldeans and settled in Harran. After the death of his father Terah, Yahweh sent him to the land of Canaan. He gave him no inheritance, not even enough ground to set his foot on. But God promised Abraham that he and his descendants would possess the land, even though at that time Abraham had no child. God spoke to him in this way: 'For four hundred years your descendants (the Israelites) will be strangers in a foreign country where they become slaves. But I will punish that nation,' God said, 'and afterward they will come out of that country and worship Me in this place.' Then He gave Abraham the covenant of circumcision. And Abraham became the father of Isaac and circumcized him eight days after his birth. Later, Isaac became the father of Jacob, and Jacob became the father of the twelve tribes of Israel.

Bible quiz: Abraham
1. Haran
2. Terah
3. Sarai (Sarah)
4. Land of Canaan
5. Fought to save him
6. Bread and wine
7. Father of the multitude
8. 100 years
9. Isaac
10. Land of Egypt

Bible word search: Abraham's faithfulness

Coloring worksheet: The call of Abram
1. God told Abram to leave his country and go to an unknown land
2. Sarai, Lot and the people that had acquired in Haran traveled to the land of Canaan with Abraham
3. Abraham and Sarah went to the land of Egypt because there was famine in the land

Lesson Eight: Gentleness
What's the Word: Opposing authority

Miriam and Aaron spoke against Moses because of the Cushite woman whom he had married; for he had married a Cushite woman. They said, "Has Yahweh indeed spoken only with Moses? Hasn't he spoken also with us?" And Yahweh heard it. Now the man Moses was very humble, more than all the men who were on the surface of the earth. Yahweh spoke suddenly to Moses, to Aaron, and to Miriam, "You three come out to the Tent of Meeting!" The three of them came out. Yahweh came down in a pillar of cloud, and stood at the door of the Tent, and called Aaron and Miriam; and they both came forward. He said, "Now hear my words. If there is a prophet among you, I, Yahweh, will make myself known to him in a vision. I will speak with him in a dream. My servant Moses is not so. He is faithful in all my house. With him, I will speak mouth to mouth, even plainly, and not in riddles; and he shall see Yahweh's form. Why then were you not afraid to speak against my servant, against Moses?" Yahweh's anger burned against them; and He departed.

Bible quiz: Aaron and Miriam oppose Moses
1. Brother and sister
2. Moses had married Cushite (Ethiopian) woman
3. All the people on the face of the earth
4. The tabernacle (tent of meeting)
5. In a pillar of cloud
6. Clearly and not in riddles
7. She became leprous
8. Heal Miriam
9. He told Moses that Miriam should be shut outside the camp
10. Seven days

Bible word search: The gentle leader

Worksheet: The tabernacle
1. For God to dwell among His people
2. Bezalel and Oholiab
3. Pure olive oil was used to light the lamps and keep them burning
4. The Israelites used the brazen altar to burn offerings and sacrifices
5. The mercy seat was on top of the ark of the covenant

Worksheet: The power of gentleness
1. Miriam and Aaron opposed Moses because they felt envy towards him for marrying a Cushite woman and questioned why Moses held all the authority
2. God declared that Moses had a unique and direct connection with Him, speaking to Moses directly, which set him apart from other prophets who received messages through dreams or visions
3. God responded to Miriam's actions by causing her to become leprous, with her skin turning as white as snow, as a visible sign of her transgression
4. Miriam was put outside the camp for seven days as a consequence of her actions. After Moses pleaded with God, she was eventually healed and her health restored

Bible craft: Make your own lapbook
Suggested Bible verses:
Love: 1 Corinthians 13:4-8
Joy: Galatians 5:22-23
Peace: John 14:27
Patience: Proverbs 16:32
Kindness: Colossians 3:12
Goodness: Psalm 73:1
Faithfulness: Matthew 25:21
Gentleness: Matthew 11:29
Self-control: Proverbs 25:28

Lesson Nine: Self-control
What's the Word: Mercy in the wilderness

When Saul returned from following the Philistines, he was told, "Behold, David is in the wilderness of Engedi." Saul took three thousand chosen men out of all Israel and went to find David and his men in front of the Wildgoats' Rocks. He came to the sheepfolds where there was a cave, and went in to relieve himself. Now David and his men were sitting in the innermost parts of the cave. And David's men said to him, "Here is the day of which God said to you, 'Behold, I will give your enemy into your hand, and you shall do to him as it shall seem good to you.'" Then David arose and stealthily cut off a corner of Saul's

robe. But afterwards, David's heart struck him because he had cut off a corner of Saul's robe. He said to his men, "God forbid that I should do this thing to my lord, who is God's anointed, to put my hand against him, seeing he is God's anointed." David persuaded his men with these words and did not permit them to attack Saul. And Saul left the cave and went on his way.

Bible quiz: David spares Saul's life
1. Following the Philistines
2. Three thousand men out of all Israel
3. To relieve himself
4. In the innermost parts of the cave
5. Cut off a corner of Saul's robe
6. Attack Saul
7. Bowed his face to the earth and paid Saul respect
8. He wept
9. Kingdom of Israel
10. Saul went home and David went up to the stronghold

Bible word search: David spares Saul's life

Coloring worksheet: David's test of self-control
1. In a cave
2. Cut off a corner of his robe
3. Saul was God's anointed king

Comprehension worksheet: Who was King Saul?
1. Saul's kingdom included the territory of Benjamin and the central highlands of Israel
2. Ask children to answer this question

Bible verse puzzle: Do you have self-control?
"A man without self-control is like a city broken into and left without walls." (Proverbs 25:28 ESV)

Worksheet: Self-control superheroes!
Questions:
1. David's men believed it was the perfect opportunity to harm King Saul because they interpreted it as a fulfillment of God's words, which promised to give David's enemy into his hand (1 Samuel 24:4)
2. David felt guilty after cutting off a piece of King Saul's robe because he realized that even that small act of harming Saul, who was anointed by God, went against his respect for God's anointed and was a breach of his loyalty (1 Samuel 24:5-6)
3. David chose not to harm King Saul because he recognized Saul as God's anointed king of Israel, and believed it was not his place to harm or act against him. David respected the position of authority that Saul held and understood that it was for God to judge and deal with Saul (1 Samuel 24:6, 10)
4. King Saul acknowledged that David had treated him well and admitted that David was more righteous than he was. Saul expressed remorse for his previous actions and recognized that David would eventually become king (1 Samuel 24:16-20)

Practising self-control:
1. Joseph resisted the advances of Potiphar's wife, even though it would have been easy for him to give in to temptation. His decision to flee from her demonstrated his strength of character and commitment to do what was right (Genesis 39:7-12)
2. Daniel displayed self-control in his dietary choices when he and his friends were taken captive in Babylon. Despite being offered rich food from the king's table, he chose to eat only vegetables and drink water (Daniel 1:8-16)
3. Yeshua displayed self-control throughout his life, especially during His trials and temptations in the desert. He resisted Satan's offers of power, fame, and pleasure, staying focused on His mission and God's Will (Matthew 4:1-11)
4. Esther demonstrated self-control by planning her approach to King Xerxes to save her people from destruction. She patiently waited for the right moment to make her request, not rushing or acting impulsively (Esther 4-5)
5. The apostle Paul exhibited self-control in his perseverance and endurance amidst challenges and persecution. He endured hardships, beatings, and imprisonments all while remaining steadfast in his faith and commitment to spreading the gospel (2 Corinthians 6:3-10, 2 Timothy 4:7)

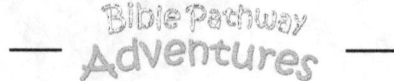

◇ DISCOVER MORE ACTIVITY BOOKS! ◇

Available for purchase at shop.biblepathwayadventures.com

INSTANT DOWNLOAD!

100 Bible Quizzes	Bereshit / Genesis
Fruit of the Spirit	Moses Ten Plagues
Twelve Tribes of Israel	Birth of The King
Women of the Bible	Fruit of the Spirit (Beginners)

www.ingramcontent.com/pod-product-compliance
Lightning Source LLC
Chambersburg PA
CBHW081429070526
44586CB00020B/2527